GOVERNMENT PROCEDURES AND OPERATIONS

MEMBERSHIP IN THE UNITED NATIONS AND ITS SPECIALIZED AGENCIES

ANALYSIS WITH SELECT COVERAGE OF UNESCO AND THE IMF

Government Procedures and Operations

Additional books in this series can be found on Nova's website under the Series tab.

Additional e-books in this series can be found on Nova's website under the e-book tab.

GOVERNMENT PROCEDURES AND OPERATIONS

MEMBERSHIP IN THE UNITED NATIONS AND ITS SPECIALIZED AGENCIES

ANALYSIS WITH SELECT COVERAGE OF UNESCO AND THE IMF

ELIZABETH SAUNDERS
EDITOR

nova publishers
New York

For permission to use material from this book please contact us:
Telephone 631-231-7269; Fax 631-231-8175
Web Site: http://www.novapublishers.com

NOTICE TO THE READER

The Publisher has taken reasonable care in the preparation of this book, but makes no expressed or implied warranty of any kind and assumes no responsibility for any errors or omissions. No liability is assumed for incidental or consequential damages in connection with or arising out of information contained in this book. The Publisher shall not be liable for any special, consequential, or exemplary damages resulting, in whole or in part, from the readers' use of, or reliance upon, this material. Any parts of this book based on government reports are so indicated and copyright is claimed for those parts to the extent applicable to compilations of such works.

Independent verification should be sought for any data, advice or recommendations contained in this book. In addition, no responsibility is assumed by the publisher for any injury and/or damage to persons or property arising from any methods, products, instructions, ideas or otherwise contained in this publication.

This publication is designed to provide accurate and authoritative information with regard to the subject matter covered herein. It is sold with the clear understanding that the Publisher is not engaged in rendering legal or any other professional services. If legal or any other expert assistance is required, the services of a competent person should be sought. FROM A DECLARATION OF PARTICIPANTS JOINTLY ADOPTED BY A COMMITTEE OF THE AMERICAN BAR ASSOCIATION AND A COMMITTEE OF PUBLISHERS.

Additional color graphics may be available in the e-book version of this book.

Library of Congress Cataloging-in-Publication Data

ISBN: 978-1-63321-971-7

Published by Nova Science Publishers, Inc. † New York

CONTENTS

PREFACE

Since the United Nations (U.N.) was established in 1945, the U.S. government, including many Members of Congress, has maintained an ongoing interest in the criteria and process for membership in the United Nations and its specialized agencies. The United Nations currently has 193 member states and two observer non-member states—the Holy See (Vatican) and "Palestine." Each of the U.N. system's 15 specialized agencies—which are independent international intergovernmental organizations with their own constitutions, rules, and budgets—have different criteria and processes for membership. This book highlights key steps in the process for attaining membership in the United Nations and its specialized agencies. It discusses the capacities associated with U.N. membership and observer status, as well as criteria for and implications of membership.

Chapter 1 – Currently, the United Nations has 193 members. The organization also has two non-member observer states, the Holy See (Vatican) and "Palestine," which have standing invitations to participate as observers in the sessions and work of the U.N. General Assembly. Each of the U.N. system's 15 specialized agencies—which are independent international intergovernmental organizations with their own constitutions, rules, and budgets—have different criteria and processes for membership. This report highlights key steps in the process for attaining membership in the United Nations and its specialized agencies. It discusses the capacities associated with U.N. membership and observer status, as well as criteria for and implications of membership.

Chapter 2 – Recent international events have renewed congressional interest in the United Nations Educational, Scientific and Cultural Organization (UNESCO). UNESCO is a specialized agency of the U.N.

system that promotes collaboration among its member countries in the fields of education, natural sciences, social and human sciences, culture, and communications and information. With an annual budget of approximately $326 million, it supports nearly 2,000 staff members working at its headquarters in Paris and 65 field offices and institutes worldwide. UNESCO activities are funded through a combination of assessed contributions by member states to its regular budget, and voluntary contributions by member states and organizations.

Chapter 3 – Recent international events have renewed congressional interest in the United Nations Educational, Scientific and Cultural Organization (UNESCO). UNESCO is a specialized agency of the U.N. system that promotes collaboration among its member countries in the fields of education, natural sciences, social and human sciences, culture, and communications and information. With an annual budget of approximately $326 million, it supports nearly 2,000 staff members working at its headquarters in Paris and 65 field offices and institutes worldwide. UNESCO activities are funded through a combination of assessed contributions by member states to its regular budget, and voluntary contributions by member states and organizations.

Chapter 4 – The International Monetary Fund (IMF), conceived at the Bretton Woods conference in July 1944, is the multilateral organization focused on the international monetary system. Created in 1946 with 46 members, it has grown to include 188 countries. The IMF has six purposes that are outlined in Article I of the IMF Articles of Agreement: promoting international monetary cooperation; expanding the balanced growth of international trade; facilitating exchange rate stability; eliminating restrictions on the international flow of capital; ensuring confidence by making the general resources of the Fund temporarily available to members; and adjusting balance-of-payments imbalances in an orderly manner.

Congressional interest in IMF activities has increased since the onset of the financial crisis in 2008. IMF lending has surged in recent years, particularly in light of large recent loans to Greece, Ireland, and Portugal. In 2009, major economies agreed to substantially increase the IMF's resources and to move forward on several major reforms at the institution. These include increasing the voting share of emerging economies; revamping the IMF's lending toolkit to introduce greater flexibility and create new facilities for low-income countries; and creating a road map for resolving the fast-growing economic imbalances in the global economy between surplus and deficit countries. In late 2010, IMF members agreed to a doubling of IMF quotas, which would require congressional authorization and appropriations.

The United States was instrumental in creating the IMF and is its largest financial contributor. Since voting shares are based on financial contributions, the large U.S. voting share provides the United States veto power over major decisions at the IMF. Both the IMF and its sister organization, the World Bank, are headquartered in Washington, DC.

At the Bretton Woods conference, the IMF was tasked with coordinating the system of fixed exchange rates to help the international economy recover from two world wars and the instability in the interwar period caused by competitive devaluations and protectionist trade policies. From 1946 until 1973, the IMF managed the "par value adjustable peg" system. The U.S. dollar was fixed to gold at $35 per ounce, and all other member countries' currencies were fixed to the dollar at different rates. This system of fixed rates ended in 1973 when the United States removed itself from the gold standard.

The IMF has evolved significantly as an institution since it was created. Floating exchange rates and more open capital markets in the 1990s created a new role for the IMF—the resolution of frequent and volatile international financial crises. The Asian financial crisis of 1997-1998 and subsequent crises in Russia and Latin America revealed many weaknesses of the world monetary system, which have only become more apparent in the wake of the 2008-2009 global financial crisis and the more recent sovereign debt crises in Europe.

This report evaluates the purpose, membership, financing, and focus of the IMF's activities. It also discusses the role of Congress in shaping U.S. policy at the IMF and concludes by addressing key issues, both legislative and oversight-related, that Congress may wish to consider.

Chapter 5 – Since its establishment in 1945, the United Nations (U.N.) has undergone numerous reforms as international stakeholders seek ways to improve the efficiency and effectiveness of the U.N. system. During the past two decades, controversies such as corruption in the Iraq Oil-For-Food Program, allegations of sexual abuse by U.N. peacekeepers, and instances of waste, fraud, and abuse by U.N. staff have focused attention on the need for change and improvement of the United Nations. Many in the international community, including the United States, continue to promote substantive reforms. The second session of the 113th Congress may focus on U.N. reform as it considers appropriate levels of U.S. funding to the United Nations and monitors the progress and implementation of ongoing and previously approved reform measures.

Generally, Congress has maintained a significant interest in the overall effectiveness of the United Nations. Some Members are particularly interested in U.N. Secretariat and management reform, with a focus on improving transparency and strengthening accountability and internal oversight. In the past, Congress has enacted legislation that links U.S. funding of the United Nations to specific U.N. reform benchmarks. Supporters of this strategy contend that the United Nations has been slow to implement reforms and that linking payment of U.S. assessments to progress on U.N. reform is the most effective way to motivate member states to efficiently pursue comprehensive reform. Opponents argue that tying U.S. funding to U.N. reform may negatively impact diplomatic relations and could hinder the United States' ability to conduct foreign policy.

In: Membership in the United Nations ... ISBN: 978-1-63321-971-7
Editor: Elizabeth Saunders

Chapter 1

MEMBERSHIP IN THE UNITED NATIONS AND ITS SPECIALIZED AGENCIES*

Luisa Blanchfield and Marjorie Ann Browne

SUMMARY

Since the United Nations (U.N.) was established in 1945, the U.S. government, including many Members of Congress, has maintained an ongoing interest in the criteria and process for membership in the United Nations and its specialized agencies. The United Nations currently has 193 member states and two observer non-member states—the Holy See (Vatican) and "Palestine."

Criteria and Process

The decision to admit a state into the United Nations is made by the U.N. General Assembly on the recommendation of the U.N. Security Council, including all five permanent members (P-5): the United States, China, France, United Kingdom, and Russia. Membership is open to all "peace-loving states" that accept the obligations contained in the U.N. Charter and, in the judgment of the organization, are able and willing to carry out such obligations. Given the imprecise nature of such criteria, many member states have broadly interpreted the conditions for U.N.

* This is an edited, reformatted and augmented version of a Congressional Research Service publication, No. R43614, dated June 19, 2014.

membership. Consequently, global and domestic politics play a primary role in many membership decisions.

Each of the United Nations' 16 specialized agencies has its own constitution, rules, membership, governance, and financial resources. As such, the process and criteria for admitting new members vary depending on the organization. In 11 specialized agencies, U.N. membership gives a state access to membership in the agency without requiring its admission to be approved by the current membership. Of these 11 agencies, 3 also provide membership, without a vote, to any member of any other specialized agency. Two other specialized agencies require a separate voting process to admit new members.

U.S. Role and Policy

Decisions on U.N. membership are subject to veto by any of the P-5; thus, the United States plays a significant role in determining U.N. membership. The United States has a more limited role in U.N. specialized agencies because decisions to admit new members to these bodies are generally made by the entire membership and each member has one vote. U.S. membership decisions in both the United Nations and its specialized agencies lie primarily with the executive branch, which represents the United States in U.N. and other multilateral fora.

Although Congress often does not play a large role in determining U.N. membership, Members have sought to influence U.S. policy on the issue through legislation advocating or opposing the membership of various countries and entities—including Israel, Montenegro, Kosovo, South Africa, China/Taiwan, and the Palestine Liberation Organization (PLO). Notably, in the mid-1990s, Congress enacted two separate laws that prohibit funding to U.N. entities that (1) admit the PLO as a member, and (2) grant full membership as a state to any organization or group that does not have the internationally recognized attributes of statehood (see Section 410 of P.L. 103- 236 and Section 414 of P.L. 101-246). The United States currently withholds its assessed and voluntary contributions to the U.N. Educational, Scientific and Cultural Organization (UNESCO), which admitted Palestine as a member in 2011.

Key Issues

Members of Congress may consider the following issues related to U.N. membership:

- **Impact on other U.N. entities and international organizations**. Membership in one U.N. organization can potentially affect membership in other U.N. entities. Some experts also suggest that U.N. membership could affect membership in other international organizations, such as the International Criminal Court.
- **U.S. contributions to U.N. entities**. Based on restrictions in U.S. law, Palestinian membership in U.N. bodies could have implications for U.S. funding of the United Nations and its specialized agencies. For example, when Palestine was admitted to UNESCO, it became eligible for membership, without a vote, in three specialized agencies—the International Fund for Agricultural Development (IFAD), the World Intellectual Property Organization (WIPO), and the U.N. Industrial Development Organization (UNIDO). To date, Palestine has not joined any of these specialized agencies. The United States is a member of IFAD and WIPO, but not UNIDO.
- **Political considerations in membership criteria and process**. Many experts agree that each U.N. member state's decision to admit a new state is largely political. The extent to which the criteria outlined in the U.N. Charter has been applied to membership applications has often depended on geopolitical issues at the time, and member states' national self-interests and views on the role and nature of the United Nations.

INTRODUCTION

Membership in the United Nations (U.N.) has been an issue of ongoing interest for Congress. Over the years, Members have focused on the process and criteria for U.N. membership, as well as on U.S. policy and roles in determining membership. Currently, the United Nations has 193 members. The organization also has two non-member observer states, the Holy See (Vatican) and "Palestine," which have standing invitations to participate as observers in the sessions and work of the U.N. General Assembly.[1] Each of the U.N. system's 15 specialized agencies—which are independent international intergovernmental organizations with their own constitutions, rules, and budgets—have different criteria and processes for membership. Examples of specialized agencies include the Food and Agriculture Organization (FAO), U.N. Educational Scientific, and Cultural Organization (UNESCO), and World Health Organization (WHO).[2]

Under Article 4 of the U.N. Charter, the U.N. Security Council and U.N. General Assembly are the primary bodies involved in the process for considering U.N. membership applications. Security Council recommendations on membership are subject to veto by any of the five permanent members. As a member of the P-5, the United States plays a key role in determining U.N. membership. It has less influence on membership decisions in the U.N. specialized agencies, where each member country has one vote and there is no veto power.

The United States & the United Nations

The United States supports the mission and mandate of the United Nations. It played a key role in establishing the organization in 1945, and serves as one of five permanent members on the Security Council.

As the single largest financial contributor to the U.N. system—assessed at 22% of the U.N. regular budget— the United States has an interest in ensuring the United Nations operates as efficiently and effectively as possible. Congress authorizes and appropriates U.S. funds to the organization each fiscal year and often uses U.N. mechanisms—particularly those related to the maintenance of international peace and security and development—to further U.S. foreign policy objectives. At the same time, many Members have also been critical of the United Nations, and have called for sweeping reform of its management and organizational structure.[3]

Any position on membership the United States takes in both the United Nations and its specialized agencies lies primarily with the executive branch, which represents the United States in U.N. fora. Generally, congressional activities related to U.N. membership have focused on supporting or opposing the membership of specific states or groups—including Israel, Kosovo, Montenegro, the Palestine Liberation Organization (PLO), South Africa, and Taiwan, among others.

This report highlights key steps in the process for attaining membership in the United Nations and its specialized agencies. It discusses the capacities associated with U.N. membership and observer status, as well as criteria for and implications of membership. It also examines related U.S. legislation and recent congressional and Obama Administration actions.

BACKGROUND

The criteria and process for admitting new U.N. members were established in 1945 by the 51 original members of the United Nations in Article 4 of the U.N. Charter.[4] U.N. membership decisions are determined by the General Assembly on the recommendation of the Security Council.[5] Membership is open to all "peace-loving states" that accept the obligations contained in the Charter and, in the judgment of the organization, are able and willing to carry out such obligations. Many experts contend that the imprecise nature of these criteria has allowed member states to broadly interpret the conditions for membership, in some cases causing political considerations to have significant weight on membership decisions.[6]

The pace at which new members have been admitted to the United Nations has generally reflected the geo-political circumstances of the time. For example, Cold War tensions contributed to the limited number of new members admitted during the organization's first decade. Both Eastern and Western bloc countries were concerned that new members might strengthen the voting power of the other bloc; consequently, just nine states were admitted between 1945 and 1954 (see **Figure 1**). From the mid-1950s through the 1970s, U.N. membership more than doubled as former European colonies in Africa were admitted. Another wave of new members resulted from the dissolution of the former Soviet Union, Yugoslavia, and Czechoslovakia in the 1990s and early 2000s. The four states most recently admitted as members were Switzerland (2002), Timor-Leste (2002), Montenegro (2006), and South Sudan (2011).

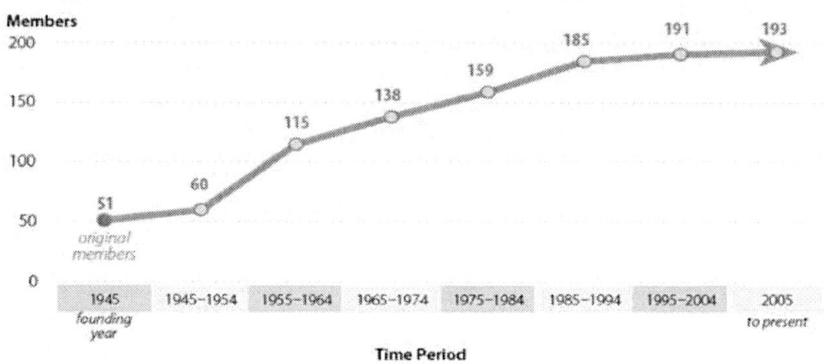

Source: United Nations, adapted by CRS.

Figure 1. U.N. Membership Growth, 1945–Present.

A key area of ongoing debate regarding U.N. membership is the organization's possible role in determining statehood. By international practice, a state is generally understood to be "an entity that has a defined territory and a permanent population, under the control of its own government, and that engages in, or has the capacity to engage in, formal relations with other such entities."[7] On the one hand, the United Nations—as an organization of independent states—does not recognize states; rather, states recognize states. As such, many experts and observers, including the United Nations itself, argue that the organization does not have the authority to recognize either a state or government.[8] On the other hand, many analysts agree that U.N. membership is an acknowledgement by U.N. members that an entity has satisfied the requirements of statehood. It provides governments with legitimacy, not only internationally, but also domestically. For many countries, membership in the United Nations provides an equal voice in U.N. bodies like the General Assembly, an international platform to advocate and pursue national and foreign policy objectives, and the opportunity to receive or provide technical or development assistance through multilateral mechanisms. Consequently, obtaining U.N. membership is often a priority for new countries, territories, organizations, or entities (hereinafter referred to as "entities" for the purpose of this report) aiming to obtain statehood.[9]

PATHS TO U.N. MEMBERSHIP: CRITERIA AND PROCESS

The circumstances under which a state obtains U.N. membership can vary. The original 51 members of the organization include many of the Allied nations of World War II that had either signed the United Nations Declaration in 1942, or participated in the founding United Nations Conference in San Francisco in 1945. The remaining 142 members were accepted for membership under the criteria and processes outlined in the Charter and the Rules of Procedure for both the General Assembly and the Security Council. Examples of circumstances under which these states obtained U.N. membership are described below, and in some cases may overlap.[10]

- Some members, sometimes referred to as **existing states**, were not among the original 51 U.N. members; they were, however, subsequently admitted to the organization. Examples include Barbados, Brazil, Italy, Japan, Tunisia, and Nigeria.

- Other members are or were **divided states**. Such states, which were divided because of the East-West conflict, have generally obtained U.N. membership after the claims of various sides had been determined in favor of either division or reunification.[11] Examples include the Federal Republic of Germany and the German Democratic Republic (now Germany), North and South Korea, and the Republic of Vietnam and Democratic Republic of Vietnam (now Vietnam).
- Some members have been admitted after the **secession or partition of a state** that was already a U.N. member. In such cases, the seceding entity reapplied for membership. Examples include the partitions of Pakistan and India and Pakistan and Bangladesh, and the admission of Estonia, Latvia, and Lithuania as new U.N. members after the breakup of the Soviet Union.
- In some cases, **two existing member states have merged**. In practice, the process for admitting such members has been flexible; the newly merged states did not have to reapply for membership. Examples include East and West Germany (Germany) and the Yemen Arab Republic and the People's Democratic Republic of Yemen (Yemen).
- One state, Indonesia, **withdrew and re-entered** the United Nations in the mid-1960s. The General Assembly and Security Council treated the withdrawal as if it were a "temporary 'inactive' membership" that ended cooperation with the organization, rather than the country's membership. The Assembly and Council provided a standing invitation for Indonesia to "reactivate" its membership at any time. Indonesia eventually rejoined the organization without reapplying for admission.[12]

U.N. Charter: Article 4

1. Membership in the United Nations is open to all other peace-loving states which accept the obligations contained in the present Charter and, in the judgment of the Organization, are able and willing to carry out these obligations.*

2. The admission of any such state to membership in the United Nations will be effected by a decision of the General Assembly upon the recommendation of the Security Council.

* *The reference to "All other peace-loving states," refers to those states applying for membership after the 51 original members of the United Nations.*

Criteria

The criteria for U.N. membership are outlined in Article 4 of the U.N. Charter (see **text box**), and can be divided into four key elements. First, an applicant must be a state. An entity applying for U.N. membership must meet the requirements of statehood under international law (a defined territory, a permanent population, and independent governance), be recognized by other states, and have the capacity to conduct diplomacy with other countries.[13]

Second, an applicant must be "peace-loving." This criterion has been used to evaluate an applicant's past and current conduct. The concept of a "peace-loving" state in many ways reflects the United Nations' purpose of maintaining international peace and security.[14]

Third, an applicant must declare that it accepts obligations contained in the U.N. Charter by (1) consenting to be bound by the U.N. Charter, a legally binding international treaty; and (2) attaching a formal declaration to its U.N. membership application.[15]

Fourth, an applicant must be willing and able to carry out U.N. Charter obligations. U.N. members have identified several indicators to consider when evaluating this criteria application: including the maintenance of friendly relations with other states; the fulfillment of international obligations; and the use of peaceful dispute settlement under international law.[16]

Process

The Security Council and General Assembly are the primary bodies that consider U.N. membership applications under Article 4 of the U.N. Charter. The rules of procedure for both the Security Council and the General Assembly set forth the details of this process. Applications for membership are submitted by the requesting state to the U.N. Secretary-General, who then forwards them to the Assembly and the Council. The amount of time it takes for an application to move through the process varies. In some cases, membership may be granted within weeks or months, while in other cases an application may remain pending indefinitely.

Role of the Security Council

When applying for U.N. membership, an applicant states that "it accepts the obligations contained in the Charter," in accordance with Rules 58 through 60 of the *Provisional Rules of Procedure of the Security Council.* The Council

President, in most instances, refers the application to the Council Committee on the Admission of New Members for its consideration.[17] The Council Committee then completes its review and submits a report, with recommended resolution language, to the Council. In a formal meeting, the Council considers the application.

Decisions on membership applications may be vetoed by any of the P-5. If the Council, however, decides to recommend the application for admission, it adopts a resolution of recommendation that is forwarded to the General Assembly, with a complete record of the discussion.[18] The Council, in recent years, has also issued a presidential statement on its action. If the Council does not recommend membership, "it shall submit a special report to the General Assembly" with a complete record of the discussion.[19]

Role of the General Assembly

Rule 136 of the *Rules of Procedure of the General Assembly* states that if the Security Council recommends the applicant state for membership, the General Assembly shall consider whether the applicant is "a peace-loving State" and is "able and willing" to carry out the obligations contained in the Charter. The Assembly decides, by a two-thirds majority of the members present and voting, on the state's application for membership. Membership becomes effective on the date on which the General Assembly adopts the resolution on admission.[20]

International Court of Justice Advisory Opinion: Role of the General Assembly Absent a Security Council Recommendation

Since the establishment of the United Nations, many governments and experts have questioned whether the General Assembly can admit a state into the United Nations without a prior Security Council resolution recommending admission. The issue became particularly pressing between 1946 and 1949, when the Security Council was unable to recommend admission for a number of states because the then-Soviet Union exercised its veto in 23 votes on membership involving at least nine states. The General Assembly sought to address the situation in 1949, when it requested the International Court of Justice (ICJ or World Court) to provide an advisory opinion on the issue.[21] In 1950, the Court ruled, by a vote of 12 to 2, that the General Assembly could not circumvent the requirement for a Security Council recommendation.[22]

If the Security Council has not recommended an application for membership or postpones its consideration, then General Assembly Rule 137 provides that the Assembly may, after full consideration of the special report of the Security Council, send the application back to the Council, along with a full record of the discussion in the Assembly, for further consideration and recommendation.

Suspension or Loss of Membership

The U.N. Charter outlines the process and criteria for suspension and loss of membership. Both actions require approval from the Security Council and the General Assembly, making them intentionally difficult to implement. Suspension is specifically addressed in Article 5, which states that U.N. members against which preventative or enforcement action has been taken by the Security Council may be suspended from the "exercise of rights and privileges" of membership. Suspension is generally not permanent; a state that is suspended remains a member and continues to be bound by obligations under the U.N. Charter.[23] Suspension requires a two-thirds majority decision by the General Assembly, on the recommendation of nine Security Council members, including the P-5. The Security Council decides whether to restore the rights and privileges of membership, also by a vote of nine in favor, including members of the P-5.[24] To date, no state has been suspended.

Loss of membership is addressed in Article 6 of the Charter. A member that has "persistently violated" the principles of the U.N. Charter may be expelled from the organization by the General Assembly on the recommendation of the Security Council. The expulsion of a member requires a two-thirds majority decision by the General Assembly, on the recommendation of nine Security Council members, including the P-5. Loss of membership is permanent; a member expelled under Article 6 is no longer bound under the obligations of the Charter. No member has been expelled to date. Instead of suspending or removing a state, members have exercised alternative measures, including

- enforcement powers under Chapter VII of the U.N. Charter, Action with Respect to Threats to the Peace, Breaches of the Peace, and Acts of Aggression;

- application of Article 19 of the Charter, which states that a U.N. member that is in financial arrears shall have no vote in the General Assembly;[25] and
- rejection of a member state's credentials in the General Assembly.[26]

U.N. Non-member Observer States

Over time, U.N. members have developed the practice of inviting entities and "non-member states" to observe the work of the United Nations, particularly the General Assembly.[27] This practice is not outlined in the U.N. Charter; rather, it has evolved in practice over many years, originating with Switzerland's application for permanent observer status in 1946. Many states that were once U.N. observers, such as Austria, Bangladesh, Japan, Switzerland, and Vietnam, eventually applied for and obtained U.N. membership. There are currently two non-member observer states: the Holy See (Vatican), which gained permanent observer status in 1964; and "Palestine," which gained observer "entity" status in 1964, and observer "non-member state" status in 2012.

MEMBERSHIP IN U.N. SPECIALIZED AGENCIES

The process and criteria for membership in U.N. specialized agencies vary depending on the organization. There are currently 15 specialized agencies in the U.N. system (see **text box**). Each of these entities is a legally independent intergovernmental organization with its own constitution, rules, membership, organs, and financial resources.

U.N. Specialized Agencies

Food and Agriculture Organization (FAO)
International Atomic Energy Agency (IAEA)[28]
International Civil Aviation Organization (ICAO)
International Labor Organization (ILO)
International Maritime Organization (IMO)
International Monetary Fund (IMF)
International Telecommunication Union (ITU)

(Continued)

International Fund for Agricultural Development (IFAD)
U.N. Educational, Scientific and Cultural Organization (UNESCO)
U.N. Industrial Development Organization (UNIDO)
U.N. World Tourism Organization (UNWTO)
Universal Postal Union (UPU)
World Bank Group (WBG)
World Health Organization (WHO)
World Intellectual Property Organization (WIPO)
World Meteorological Organization (WMO)

The United States is a member of all specialized agencies except for two—UNIDO and UNWTO. The membership requirements set forth in the constitutions of these agencies show a range of membership processes, summarized below (also see the **Appendix**).

- In 11 specialized agencies, membership in the United Nations gives a state access to membership in the agency without having to have its admission approved by the membership of the agency (ICAO, IFAD, ILO, IMO, ITU, UNIDO, UPU, WHO, WIPO, WMO, and UNESCO).
  - Of these 11 agencies, three also provide membership, without a vote, to member nations of any specialized agency (IFAD, UNIDO, and WIPO).
- Two agencies require some process of voting for admission (FAO and UNWTO).
  - UNWTO requires a two-thirds vote of its General Assembly for membership—however, an amendment to Article 5 of its statute, adopted in 2005 but not yet in force, would have membership open to all states that are U.N. members.
- The two international financial institutions—the World Bank Group and the IMF—have different membership processes.
  - Each member of the IMF is assigned a quota "based broadly on its relative position in the world economy," which determines its maximum financial commitment to the IMF, voting power, and access to IMF financing.[30] In order to admit new IMF members, the overall quota must be changed. (Because the United States

currently controls 16.75 percent of IMF votes, it can block the admission of any new members.)

- To be a member of the World Bank Group, entities must also be members of the IMF. Specifically, IMF membership is required to join the Group's International Bank for Reconstruction and Development (IBRD, the Bank's non-concessional lending facility). In turn, IBRD membership is required for admission to other parts of the Group, including the International Development Association (the Bank's concessional lending facility) and the International Finance Corporation (which lends to private sector entities in development countries), among others.

Some specialized agencies allow for "associate membership." Generally, an associate member is defined as a territory or group of territories that are not responsible for the conduct of its international relations. The criteria and activities related to this type of membership vary depending on the organization and are often outlined in specialized agency constitutions, statutes, or rules of procedure.[31]

Examples of specialized agencies that grant associate membership include FAO, UNESCO, and WHO.

PALESTINIAN MEMBERSHIP EFFORTS[32]

Palestine's change in observer status and its efforts to apply for U.N. membership have garnered significant domestic and international attention. These events are part of a broader, ongoing initiative by Palestine Liberation Organization (PLO) Chairman and Palestinian Authority President Mahmoud Abbas to obtain membership or non-member observer state status in various U.N. and related bodies as a means to achieving more widespread recognition of Palestinian statehood.

Brief descriptions of these efforts follow.

- **Application for U.N. Membership**. In September 2011, Palestine submitted an application for membership to U.N. Secretary-General Ban Ki-moon. The Secretary-General subsequently submitted it to the Security Council for consideration. The Council's Committee on the Admission of New Members stated that it was "unable to make a unanimous recommendation to the Security Council" regarding Palestine's application.[33] The application remains pending and is unlikely to be considered by the Council. The Obama Administration has stated that the United States would veto any proposed Security Council resolution recommending Palestinian membership.

- **Change in U.N. Observer Status**. In November 2012, the U.N. General Assembly voted to change Palestine's observer status from "entity" to "nonmember state."[34] Palestine's previous relationship with the United Nations, as defined through a series of General Assembly resolutions, was as an observer "entity." As a permanent non-member observer state, Palestine has maintained many of the capacities it had as an entity.[35] Although Palestine has the term "state" in its current designation, it is not a U.N. member. As a non-member state, Palestine does not have the right to vote, call for a vote, or put forward candidates in the General Assembly.[36]
- **UNESCO Membership**. In October 2011, the UNESCO General Conference— the organization's main decision-making body—adopted a resolution admitting Palestine as a member. The General Conference agreed to Palestinian membership by a vote of 107 in favor, 14 against (including the United States), and 52 abstaining.
- **Accession to Multilateral Treaties**. In April 2014, the Palestinians submitted 13 letters of accession to the United Nations and two to the governments of Switzerland and Norway for a range of international convention and treaties.[37] Accession is proceeding in accordance with the specific provisions set forth in each treaty.

- **UNESCO Membership**. In October 2011, the UNESCO General Conference— the organization's main decision-making body—adopted a resolution admitting Palestine as a member. The General Conference agreed to Palestinian membership by a vote of 107 in favor, 14 against (including the United States), and 52 abstaining.
- **Accession to Multilateral Treaties**. In April 2014, the Palestinians submitted 13 letters of accession to the United Nations and two to the governments of Switzerland and Norway for a range of international convention and treaties.[37] Accession is proceeding in accordance with the specific provisions set forth in each treaty.

Palestine, the United Nations, and the International Criminal Court[38]

Some analysts have raised questions regarding the possible impact of Palestinian membership in the United Nations on the jurisdiction of the International Criminal Court (ICC; the "Court"). Under the Rome Statute, the treaty that established the ICC, only a state may submit itself to the jurisdiction of the Court. A state that is not a party to the Statute may nevertheless make an ad hoc declaration to submit its nationals or territory to the jurisdiction of the Court for a situation in which possible war crimes, crimes against humanity, or genocide might have occurred.[39]

During the December 2008-January 2009 conflict in the Gaza Strip, Israeli armed forces conducted military operations in the Gaza Strip and hostilities took place between Israeli and Palestinian forces. In the wake of the conflict, the Palestinian Authority (PA) justice minister in January 2009 submitted an ad hoc declaration to the ICC on behalf on the "Government of Palestine" asking the Court to exercise jurisdiction over "the territory of Palestine" regarding "acts" committed since July 1, 2002.[40] The ICC's Office of the Prosecutor (OTP) opened a preliminary examination in order to determine whether an investigation would proceed, including whether preconditions for the exercise of ICC jurisdiction existed.

In April 2012, the OTP issued an opinion stating that it could not exercise jurisdiction over the territory of Palestine, because it could not make the determination of whether the PA's declaration was on behalf of a state, given continued controversy surrounding the issue. The OTP stated that it could in the future consider allegations of crimes committed in Palestine if the U.N. Security Council or U.N. General Assembly took action on the issue of the statehood of Palestine, or if the Security Council made a referral to the ICC of the situation in Palestine. According to the OTP, the ICC's Assembly of States Parties (ASP) could also consider the matter.[41]

In November 2012, the General Assembly adopted a resolution according Palestine "non-member observer State status in the United Nations.... " In a November 2013 report, the OTP stated that this resolution did not make the 2009 PA ad hoc declaration valid for purposes of ICC jurisdiction, and that the OTP could not open a new preliminary examination of the situation. The OTP explained, however, that the status of Palestine as a non-member observer state in the General Assembly "is of direct relevance to the issue of the Court's jurisdiction."

Since the General Assembly's resolution, no representative of Palestine has lodged a new ad hoc declaration accepting the ICC's jurisdiction over the situation in Palestine.[42] This raises the question of whether a new Palestinian declaration either seeking to accede to the Rome Statute or recognizing the ICC's jurisdiction over territory referred to as Palestinian might be accepted in light of the change in Palestine's U.N. observer status in November 2012. Since the General Assembly's resolution, no such declaration has been made.

U.S. POLICY

As one of the five permanent members of the Security Council, the United States can play a key role in determining membership in the United Nations. It has a more limited role in determining membership in U.N. specialized agencies. A decision to admit a new member in these bodies is generally made by the entire membership, where each member—including the United States—has one vote. The decision to vote for or against membership in both the United Nations and its specialized agencies lies primarily with the executive branch of the U.S. government, which represents the United States in the United Nations and related agencies.

Members of Congress, however, have sought to influence U.S. policy on the issue by proposing legislation advocating or opposing the membership of various countries and entities—including Israel, Montenegro, Kosovo, South Africa, China/Taiwan, and the PLO. Some Members have also introduced legislation calling on the United Nations to suspend the membership of any country that does not meet certain criteria.[43] Notably, in the mid-1990s, Congress enacted two laws to prohibit funding to the United Nations or its affiliated organizations under specific conditions related to internationally recognized attributes of statehood or PLO membership in the United Nations:

- **Section 410 of the Foreign Relations Authorization Act, Fiscal Years 1994 and 1995** (P.L. 103-236) states that the United States shall not make contributions to "any affiliated organization of the United Nations which grants full membership as a state to any organization or group that does not have the internationally recognized attributes of statehood"; and
- **Section 414 of the Foreign Relations Authorization Act, Fiscal Years 1990 and 1991** (P.L. 101-246) states, "No funds authorized to

be appropriated by this Act or any other Act shall be available for the United Nations or any specialized agencies thereof which accords the Palestine Liberation Organization the same standing as member states."[44]

The United States currently withholds its voluntary and assessed contributions to UNESCO in response to the 2011 decision by UNESCO members to admit Palestine as a member.[45] In FY2013 through FY2015, the President asked Congress to provide authority to waive the above-mentioned legislative restrictions; however, many Members of Congress appear unwilling to do so.[46] The Obama Administration has stated that the United States does not intend to withdraw from UNESCO despite the funding restrictions. In November 2013, the United States lost its voting rights in the UNESCO General Conference as a result of its withholding of assessed contributions.[47]

The 113th Congress has addressed U.N. membership primarily in the context of specific countries—with a particular focus on Palestinian membership efforts. For example, the FY2014 foreign operations appropriations bill (Division K of P.L. 113-76) prohibits U.S. assistance to the Palestinian Authority if the Palestinians obtain membership in the United Nations or U.N. specialized agencies outside of an agreement negotiated between Israel and the Palestinians. The Secretary of State may waive these restrictions if he certifies to the appropriations committees that doing so is in the national security interests of the United States. In addition, Members have introduced legislation seeking to further tie U.S. funding of the United Nations to Palestinian membership decisions,[48] and expressing support for Taiwan's participation and membership in the United Nations.[49]

ISSUES FOR CONGRESS

As the 113th Congress considers issues related to membership in the United Nations and its specialized agencies, Members may take several policy issues and related questions into account.

Impact on Membership in Other U.N. Entities

U.S. decisions on membership in one U.N. entity can potentially affect membership in related U.N. entities. For instance, as discussed previously, states that are admitted as members of the United Nations are eligible for membership, without a vote, in 11 specialized agencies. Three of these specialized agencies—IFAD, UNIDO, and WIPO—offer membership, also without a vote, to members of any other specialized agency.

A newly admitted member of the United Nations, IFAD, UNIDO, or WIPO that wishes to obtain membership in specialized agencies must provide appropriate notification. The type and extent of such notifications vary depending on the organization.

U.S. Contributions to U.N. System Entities

Based on existing restrictions in U.S. law, Palestinian membership in U.N. bodies could have implications for U.S. contributions to the United Nations and its specialized agencies. When Palestine was admitted to UNESCO in October 2011, for example, it also became eligible for membership, without a vote, in IFAD, UNIDO, and WIPO. To date, the Palestinians have not pursued membership at these organizations; however, if they were to do so, they would likely receive an invitation for membership. The United States is a member of IFAD and WIPO, and is not a member of UNIDO. It is unclear whether the United States would withhold funding to these organizations as it has done in the case of UNESCO.

Role of Politics in Membership Criteria and Process

Experts and observers generally agree that individual U.N. members' response to the criteria for U.N. membership and decision to admit a state are inherently political. The extent to which the criteria have been applied to various membership applications has depended on the applicant country or entity, geopolitical issues at the time, and individual member states' national interests and views on the role and nature of the United Nations. In particular, the complex relationships among member states play an important role in membership decisions. These relationships are independent of the United Nations, but can impact whether an entity or state applies for membership, if an application is considered by the Security Council and General Assembly and, ultimately, whether an entity is invited to be a member of the organization.

Looking Ahead: Key Questions

In light of the aforementioned issues, Members of Congress may face several questions related to U.N. and specialized agency membership, including

- whether to support or oppose the efforts of various entities to pursue membership in the United Nations or its specialized agencies;
- what specific steps Members might take to support or oppose the membership of various entities, including, but not limited to, those that represent the Palestinians; and
- how, if at all, to address the Obama Administration's continued requests to support legislation that would provide authority to waive the legislative restrictions that prohibit U.S. funding for UNESCO.

The extent to which Members might address these issues depends on a range of factors— including whether the Palestinians pursue membership in other U.N. entities and how such efforts might take place within the context of overall Israeli-Palestinian relations; as well as other domestic and foreign policy priorities.

APPENDIX. MEMBERSHIP-RELATED PROVISIONS FOR U.N. SPECIALIZED AGENCIES

The table below provides relevant membership provisions for U.N. specialized agencies and one related organization. It draws from various agency constitutions, conventions, or statutes that address (1) the process and/or criteria for membership, (2) withdrawal from the organization, and (3) the impact of arrears.

Table A-1. Provisions Addressing Membership in U.N. Specialized Agencies and One Related Organization

Specialized Agency	Provisions for Membership	Provisions for Withdrawal or Arrears
Food and Agriculture Organization (FAO)*	*Constitution* Article II. 2. The Conference may by a two-thirds majority of the votes cast, provided that a majority of the Member Nations of the Organization is present, decide to admit as an additional Member ... any nation which has submitted an application for membership and a declaration made in a formal instrument that it will accept the obligations of the Constitution as in force at the time of admission.	*Constitution* Article III. 4. A. A Member Nation which is in arrears in the payment of its financial contributions to the Organization shall have no vote in the Conference if the amount of its arrears equals or exceeds the amount of the contributions due from it for the two preceding calendar years. The Conference may, nevertheless, permit such a Member Nation to vote if it is satisfied that the failure to pay is due to conditions beyond the control of the Member Nation. Article XIX. Any Member Nation may give notice of withdrawal from the Organization at any time after the expiration of four years from the date of its acceptance of this Constitution. ...Such notice shall take effect one year after the date of its communication to the Director-General. The financial obligation to the Organization of a Member Nation which has given notice of withdrawal ...shall include the entire calendar year in which the notice takes effect.

Specialized Agency	*Provisions for Membership*	*Provisions for Withdrawal or Arrears*
International Civil Aviation Organization (ICAO)*	*Convention* Article 92. (a) This Convention shall be open for adherence by members of the United Nations and States associated with them, ... (b) Adherence shall be effected by a notification addressed to the Government of the United States of America and shall take effect as from the thirtieth day from the receipt of the notification by the Government of the United States..., which shall notify all the contracting States. Article 93. States other than those provided for in Articles 91 and 92 (a) may, subject to approval by any general international organization set up by the nations of the world to preserve peace, be admitted to participation in this Convention by means of a four-fifths vote of the Assembly and on such conditions as the Assembly may prescribe....	*Convention* Article 62. The Assembly may suspend the voting power in the Assembly and in the Council of any contracting State that fails to discharge within a reasonable period its financial obligations to the Organization.
International Fund for Agricultural Development (IFAD)*	*Agreement* Article 3. Section 1. (a) Membership of the Fund shall be open to any State member of the United Nations or of any of its specialized agencies, or of the International Atomic Energy Agency. Section 2. (b) Non-original Members of the Fund shall be those other States that, after approval of their membership by the Governing Council, become parties to this Agreement in accordance with Section 1 (c) of Article 13. (Article 13. Section 1 (c).	*Agreement* Article 9. Section 1. Withdrawal. (a) Except as provided in Section 4 (a) of this Article, a Member may withdraw from the Fund by depositing an instrument of denunciation of this Agreement with the Depository. (b) Withdrawal of a Member shall take effect on the date specified in its instrument of denunciation, but in no event less than six months after deposit of such instrument. Section 2.

Table A-1. (Continued)

Specialized Agency	Provisions for Membership	Provisions for Withdrawal or Arrears
	States listed in Schedule I that have not become parties to this Agreement within one year after its entry into force and States that are not so listed, may, after approval of their membership by the Governing Council, become parties by depositing an instrument of accession.)	Suspension of Membership. (a) If a Member fails to fulfil any of its obligations to the Fund, the Governing Council may, by a three-fourths majority of the total number of votes, suspend its membership. The Member so suspended shall automatically cease to be a Member one year from the date of its suspension, unless the Council decides by the same majority of the total number of votes to restore the Member to good standing.
International Labor Organization (ILO)*	*Constitution* Article 1. 3. Any original member of the United Nations and any State admitted to membership of the United Nations by a decision of the General Assembly in accordance with the provisions of the Charter may become a Member of the International Labor Organization by communicating to the Director-General of the International Labor Office its formal acceptance of the obligations of the Constitution of the International Labor Organization. Article 1. 4.	*Constitution* Article 13. 4. A Member of the Organization which is in arrears in the payment of its financial contribution to the Organization shall have no vote in the Conference, in the Governing Body, in any committee, or in the elections of members of the Governing Body, if the amount of its arrears equals or exceeds the amount of the contributions due from it for the preceding two full years: Provided that the Conference may by a two-thirds majority of the votes cast by the delegates present permit such a Member to vote if it is satisfied that the failure to pay is due to conditions beyond the control of the Member.

Specialized Agency	Provisions for Membership	Provisions for Withdrawal or Arrears
	The General Conference of the International Labor Organization may also admit Members to the Organization by a vote concurred in by two-thirds of the delegates attending the session, including two-thirds of the Government delegates present and voting. Such admission shall take effect on the communication to the Director-General of the International Labor Office by the government of the new Member of its formal acceptance of the obligations of the Constitution of the Organization.	Article 1. 5. No Member of the International Labor Organization may withdraw from the Organization without giving notice of its intention so to do to the Director-General of the International Labor Office. Such notice shall take effect two years after the date of its reception by the Director-General, subject to the Member having at that time fulfilled all financial obligations arising out of its membership. When a Member has ratified any international labor Convention, such withdrawal shall not affect the continued validity for the period provided for in the Convention of all obligations arising thereunder or relating thereto.
International Maritime Organization (IMO)*	*Convention* Article 5. Membership in the Organization is open to all States, subject to the provisions of Part III. Article 6. Members of the United Nations may become Members of the Organization by becoming parties to the Convention in accordance with the provisions of Article 57. Article 8. Any States not entitled to become a Member under Article 6 or 7 may apply through the Secretary-General of the Organization to become a Member and shall be admitted as a Member upon its becoming a party to the Convention in accordance with the provisions of	*Convention* Article 59. (a) Any Member may withdraw from the Organization by written notification given to the Secretary-General of the United Nations, who will immediately inform the other Members and the Secretary-General of the Organization of such notification. Notification of withdrawal may be given at any time after the expiration of twelve months from the date on which the Convention has come into force. The withdrawal shall take effect upon the expiration of twelve months from the date on which such written notification is received by the Secretary-General of the United Nations.

Table A-1. (Continued)

Specialized Agency	Provisions for Membership	Provisions for Withdrawal or Arrears
	Article 57 provided that, upon the recommendation of the Council, its application has been approved by two-thirds of the Members other than Associate Members. Article 57. Subject to the provisions of Part III [on Membership] the present Convention shall remain open for signature or acceptance and States may become parties to the Convention by: (a) Signature without reservation as to acceptance; (b) Signature subject to acceptance followed by acceptance; or (c) Acceptance. Acceptance shall be affected by the deposit of an instrument with the Secretary-General of the United Nations.	Article 42. Any Member which fails to discharge its financial obligation to the Organization within one year from the date on which it is due, shall have no vote in the Assembly, the Council, or the Maritime Safety Committee unless the Assembly, at its discretion, waives this provision.
International Telecommunication Union (ITU)*	*Constitution* Article 2. It [ITU] shall ... be composed of (b) any other State, a Member of the United Nations, which accedes to this Constitution and the Convention in accordance with Article 53 of this Constitution; (c) any other State, not a Member of the United Nations, which applies for membership of the Union and which, after having secured approval of such application by two-thirds of the Member States of the Union, accedes to this Constitution and the Convention in accordance with Article 53 of this Constitution.	*Constitution* Article 28. A Member State which is in arrears in its payments to the Union shall lose its right to vote as defined in Nos. 27 and 28 of this Constitution for so long as the amount of its arrears equals or exceeds the amount of the contribution due for the two preceding years. Article 57. 1. Each Member State which has ratified, accepted, approved or acceded to this Constitution and the Convention shall have the right to denounce them.

Specialized Agency	Provisions for Membership	Provisions for Withdrawal or Arrears
		In such a case, this Constitution and the Convention shall be denounced simultaneously in one single instrument, by a notification addressed to the Secretary-General. Upon receipt of such notification, the Secretary-General shall advise the other Member States thereof. 2. Such denunciation shall take effect at the expiration of a period of one year from the date of receipt of its notification by the Secretary-General.
United Nations Educational, Scientific and Cultural Organization (UNESCO)*	*Constitution* Article 2. 1. Membership of the United Nations Organization shall carry with it the right to membership of the United Nations Educational, Scientific and Cultural Organization; 2. Subject to the conditions of the Agreement between this Organization and the United Nations Organization, approved pursuant to Article X of this Constitution, states not members of the United Nations Organization may be admitted to membership of the Organization, upon recommendation of the Executive Board, by a two-thirds majority vote of the General Conference.	*Constitution* Article 2. 4. Members of the Organization which are suspended from the exercise of the rights and privileges of membership of the United Nations Organization shall, upon the request of the latter, be suspended from the rights and privileges of this Organization; 5. Members of the Organization which are expelled from the United Nations Organization shall automatically cease to be Members of this Organization; 6. Any Member State or Associate Member of the Organization may withdraw from the Organization by notice addressed to the Director-General. Such notice shall take effect on 31 December of the year following that during which the notice was given. No such withdrawal shall affect the financial obligations owed to the Organization on the date the withdrawal takes effect.

Table A-1. (Continued)

Specialized Agency	Provisions for Membership	Provisions for Withdrawal or Arrears
		Notice of withdrawal by an Associate Member shall be given on its behalf by the Member State or other authority having responsibility for its international relations.
United Nations Industrial Development Organization (UNIDO)	*Constitution* Article 3. (a) States members of the United Nations or of a specialized agency or of the International Atomic Energy Agency may become Members of the Organization by becoming parties to this Constitution in accordance with Article 24 and paragraph 2 of Article 25; (b) States other than 'those referred to in subparagraph (a) may become Members of the Organization by becoming parties to this Constitution in accordance with paragraphs of Article 24 and subparagraph 2 (c) of Article 25, after their membership has been approved by the Conference, by a two-thirds majority of the Members present and voting, upon the recommendation of the Board.	*Constitution* Article 5. Suspension. 1. Any Member of the Organization that is suspended from the exercise of the rights and privileges of membership of the United Nations shall automatically be suspended from the exercise of the rights and privileges of membership of the Organization. Article 6. Withdrawal. 2. Any Member that is in arrears in the payment of its financial contributions to the Organization shall have no vote in the Organization if the amount of its arrears equals or exceeds the amount of the assessed contributions due from it for the preceding two fiscal years. Any organ may, nevertheless, permit such a Member to vote in that organ if it is satisfied that the failure to pay is due to conditions beyond the control of the Member.

Specialized Agency	Provisions for Membership	Provisions for Withdrawal or Arrears
Universal Postal Union (UPU)*	*Constitution* Article 11.1. Any member of the United Nations may accede to the Union; 2. Any sovereign country which is not a member of the United Nations may apply for admission as a member country of the Union; 3. Accession or application for admission to the Union must entail a formal declaration of accession to the Constitution and to the obligatory Acts of the Union. It shall be addressed by the government of the country concerned to the Director General of the International Bureau, who shall notify the accession or consult the member countries on the application for admission, as the case may be; 4. A country which is not a member of the United Nations shall be deemed to be admitted as a member country if its application is approved by at least two thirds of the member countries of the Union.	*Constitution* Article 12. 1. Each member country may withdraw from the Union by notice of denunciation of the Constitution given by the government of the country concerned to the Director General of the International Bureau and by him to the governments of member countries; 2. Withdrawal from the Union shall become effective one year after the day on which the notice of denunciation provided for in paragraph 1 is received by the Director General of the International Bureau.
World Health Organization (WHO)*	*Constitution* Article 4. Members of the United Nations may become Members of the Organization by signing or otherwise accepting this Constitution in accordance with the provisions of Chapter XIX and in accordance with their constitutional processes. Article 6. Subject to the conditions of any agreement between the United Nations and the Organization, approved pursuant to Chapter XVI, States which do not become Members in accordance with Articles 4	*Constitution* Article 7. If a Member fails to meet its financial obligations to the Organization or in other exceptional circumstances, the Health Assembly may, on such conditions as it thinks proper, suspend the voting privileges and services to which a Member is entitled. The Health Assembly shall have the authority to restore such voting privileges and services.

Table A-1. (Continued)

Specialized Agency	Provisions for Membership	Provisions for Withdrawal or Arrears
	and 5 may apply to become Members and shall be admitted as Members when their application has been approved by a simple majority vote of the Health Assembly.	
World Intellectual Property Organization (WIPO)*	*Convention* Article 5. (1) Membership in the Organization shall be open to any State which is a member of any of the Unions as defined in Article 2(vii). (2) Membership in the Organization shall be equally open to any State not a member of any of the Unions, provided that: (i) it is a member of the United Nations, any of the Specialized Agencies brought into relationship with the United Nations, or the International Atomic Energy Agency, or is a party to the Statute of the International Court of Justice, or it is invited by the General Assembly to become a party to this Convention.	*Convention* Article 11. 5. Any State party to this [WIPO] Convention not member of any of the Unions which is in arrears in the payment of its financial contributions under the present Article, and any State party to this Convention member of any of the Unions which is in arrears in the payment of its contributions to any of the Unions, shall have no vote in any of the bodies of the Organization of which it is a member, if the amount of its arrears equals or exceeds the amount of the contributions due from it for the preceding two full years. However, any of these bodies may allow such a State to continue to exercise its vote in that body if, and as long as, it is satisfied that the delay in payment arises from exceptional and unavoidable circumstances.

Specialized Agency	Provisions for Membership	Provisions for Withdrawal or Arrears
World Meteorological Organization (WMO)*	*Convention* Article 3. The following may become Members of the Organization by the procedure set forth in the present Convention ... (b) Any Member of the United Nations having a meteorological service by acceding to the present Convention in accordance with Article 33; (c) Any State, fully responsible for the conduct of its international relations and having a meteorological service, not listed in Annex I of the present Convention and not a Member of the United Nations, after the submission of a request for membership to the Secretariat of the Organization and after its approval by two-thirds of the Members of the Organization as specified in paragraphs (a), (b) and (c) of this Article by acceding to the present Convention...	*Convention* Article 30. (a) Any Member may withdraw from the Organization on twelve months' notice in writing given by it to the Secretary General of the Organization, who shall at once inform all the Members of the Organization of such notice of withdrawal; (b) Any Member of the Organization not responsible for its own international relations may be withdrawn from the Organization on twelve months' notice in writing given by the Member or other authority responsible for its international relations to the Secretary General of the Organization, who shall at once inform all the Members of the Organization of such notice of withdrawal. Article 31. If any Member fails to meet its financial obligations to the Organization or otherwise fails in its obligations under the present Convention, the Congress may by resolution suspend it from exercising its rights and enjoying privileges as a Member of the Organization until it has met such financial or other obligations.

Table A-1. (Continued)

Specialized Agency	Provisions for Membership	Provisions for Withdrawal or Arrears
World Tourism Organization (UNWTO)	*Statute* Article 5. Full membership of the Organization shall be open to all sovereign States ... 3. Other States may become Full Members of the Organization if their candidatures are approved by the General Assembly by a majority of two-thirds of the Full Members present and voting provided that said majority is a majority of the Full Members of the Organization.	*Statute* Article 35. 1. Any Full Member may withdraw from the Organization on the expiry of one year's notice in writing to the Depositary Government. Annex. 13. A Member which is in arrears in the payment of its financial contributions to the Organization's expenditure shall be deprived of the privileges enjoyed by the Members in the form of services and the right to vote in the Assembly and the Council if the amount of its arrears equals or exceeds the amount of the contributions due from it for the preceding two financial years. At the request of the Council, the Assembly may, however, permit such a Member to vote and to enjoy the services of the Organization if it is satisfied that the failure to pay is due to conditions beyond the control of the Member.
International Monetary Fund (IMF)*	*Articles of Agreement* Article II. Membership shall be open to other countries at such times and in accordance with such terms as may be prescribed by the Board of Governors.	*Articles of Agreement* Article XXVI: Withdrawal from Membership - Section 1. Right of members to withdraw: Any member may withdraw from the Fund at any time by transmitting a notice in writing to the Fund at its principal office. Withdrawal shall become effective on the date such notice is received.

Specialized Agency	*Provisions for Membership*	*Provisions for Withdrawal or Arrears*
	These terms, including the terms for subscriptions, shall be based on principles consistent with those applied to other countries that are already members.	Section 2. Compulsory withdrawal: (a) If a member fails to fulfill any of its obligations under this Agreement, the Fund may declare the member ineligible to use the general resources of the Fund. Nothing in this Section shall be deemed to limit the provisions of Article V, Section 5 or Article VI, Section 1. (b) If, after the expiration of a reasonable period following a declaration of ineligibility under (a) above, the member persists in its failure to fulfill any of its obligations under this Agreement, the Fund may, by a seventy percent majority of the total voting power, suspend the voting rights of the member. During the period of the suspension, the provisions of Schedule L shall apply. The Fund may, by a seventy percent majority of the total voting power, terminate the suspension at any time. (c) If, after the expiration of a reasonable period following a decision of suspension under (b) above, the member persists in its failure to fulfill any of its obligations under this Agreement, that member may be required to withdraw from membership in the Fund by a decision of the Board of Governors carried by a majority of the Governors having eighty-five percent of the total voting power.

Table A-1. (Continued)

Specialized Agency	Provisions for Membership	Provisions for Withdrawal or Arrears
		(d) Regulations shall be adopted to ensure that before action is taken against any member under (a), (b), or (c) above, the member shall be informed in reasonable time of the complaint against it and given an adequate opportunity for stating its case, both orally and in writing.
World Bank Group* International Bank for Reconstruction and Development (IBRD)	*IBRD (the Bank), Articles of Agreement* Article II, Section 1 (a) The original members of the Bank shall be those members of the International Monetary Fund which accept membership in the Bank before the date specified... (b) Membership shall be open to other members of the Fund, at such times and in accordance with such terms as may be prescribed by the Bank.	*IBRD (the Bank), Articles of Agreement* Article VI. Section 1. Right of Members to Withdraw. Any member may withdraw from the Bank at any time by transmitting a notice in writing to the Bank at its principal office. Withdrawal shall become effective on the date such notice is received. Section 2. Suspension of Membership. If a member fails to fulfill any of its obligations to the Bank, the Bank may suspend its membership by decision of a majority of the Governors, exercising a majority of the total voting power. The member so suspended shall automatically cease to be a member one year from the date of its suspension unless a decision is taken by the same majority to restore the member to good standing. While under suspension, a member shall not be entitled to exercise any rights under this Agreement, except the right of withdrawal, but shall remain subject to all obligations.

Specialized Agency	Provisions for Membership	Provisions for Withdrawal or Arrears
International Development Association (IDA)	*IDA, Articles of Agreement* Article II, Section 1 (a) The original members of the Association shall be those members of the Bank (IBRD) listed in Schedule A hereto which, on or before the date specified ... accept membership in the Association. (b) Membership shall be open to other members of the Bank at such times and in accordance with such terms as the Association may determine.	*IDA, Articles of Agreement* Article VII. Section 1. Withdrawal by Members. Any member may withdraw from membership in the Association at any time by transmitting, a notice in writing to the Association at its principal office. Withdrawal shall become effective upon the date such notice is received. Section 2. Suspension of Membership. (a) If a member fails to fulfill any of its obligations to the Association, the Association may suspend its membership by decision of a majority of the Governors, exercising a majority of the total voting power. The member so suspended shall automatically cease to be a member one year from the date of its suspension unless a decision is taken by the same majority to restore the member to good standing. (b) While under suspension, a member shall not be entitled to exercise any rights under this Agreement except the right of withdrawal, but shall remain subject to all obligations. Section 3. Suspension or Cessation of Membership in the Bank. Any member which is suspended from membership in, or ceases to be a member of, the Bank shall automatically be suspended from membership in, or cease to be a member of, the Association, as the case may be.

Table A-1. (Continued)

Specialized Agency	Provisions for Membership	Provisions for Withdrawal or Arrears
International Finance Corporation (IFC)	*IFC, Articles of Agreement* Article II, Section 1 (a) The original members of the Corporation shall be those members of the Bank (IBRD) listed in Schedule A hereto which shall, on or before the date specified ... (c), accept membership in the Corporation. (b) Membership shall be open to other members of the Bank at such times and in accordance with such terms as may be prescribed by the Corporation.	*IFC, Articles of Agreement* Article V. Section 1.Withdrawal by Members (1) Any member may withdraw from membership in the Corporation at any time by transmitting a notice in writing to the Corporation at its principal office. Withdrawal shall become effective upon the date such notice is received. Section 2. Suspension of Membership. (a) If a member fails to fulfill any of its obligations to the Corporation, the Corporation may suspend its membership by decision of a majority of the Governors, exercising a majority of the total voting power. The member so suspended shall automatically cease to be a member one year from the date of its suspension unless a decision is taken by the same majority to restore the member to good standing. (b) While under suspension, a member shall not be entitled to exercise any rights under this Agreement except the right of withdrawal, but shall remain subject to all obligations. Section 3. Suspension or Cessation of Membership in the Bank (IRBD).

Specialized Agency	Provisions for Membership	Provisions for Withdrawal or Arrears
		Any member which is suspended from membership in, or ceases to be a member of, the Bank shall automatically be suspended from membership in, or cease to be a member of, the Corporation, as the case may be.
Multilateral Investment Guarantee Agency (MIGA)	*MIGA, Convention*	*MIGA, Convention*
	Article 4 (a) Membership in the Agency shall be open to all members of the Bank and to Switzerland.	Article 51. Withdrawal. Any member may, after the expiration of three years following the date upon which this Convention has entered into force with respect to such member, withdraw from the Agency at any time by giving notice in writing to the Agency at its principal office. Article 52. Suspension of membership. If a member fails to fulfill any of its obligations under this Convention, the Council may, by a majority of its members exercising a majority of the total voting power, suspend its membership.
International Centre for Settlement of Investments and Disputes (ICSID)	*ICSID, Convention* Article 67. This Convention shall be open for signature on behalf of States members of the Bank. It shall also be open for signature on behalf of any other State which is a party to the Statute of the International Court of Justice and which the Administrative Council, by a vote of two-thirds of its members, shall have invited to sign the Convention.	*ICSID, Convention* Article 71. Any Contracting State may denounce this Convention by written notice to the depositary of this Convention. The denunciation shall take effect six months after receipt of such notice.

Table A-1. (Continued)

Specialized Agency	Provisions for Membership	Provisions for Withdrawal or Arrears
RELATED ORGANIZATION (NOT A SPECIALIZED AGENCY)		
International Atomic Energy Agency (IAEA)*	*Statute* Article IV. B. Other members of the Agency shall be those States, whether or not Members of the United Nations or of any of the specialized agencies, which deposit an instrument of acceptance of this Statute after their membership has been approved by the General Conference upon the recommendation of the Board of Governors. In recommending and approving a State for membership, the Board of Governors and the General Conference shall determine that the State is able and willing to carry out the obligations of membership in the Agency, giving due consideration to its ability and willingness to act in accordance with the purposes and principles of the Charter of the United Nations.	*Statute* Article XVII. D. At any time after five years from the date when this Statute shall take effect in accordance with paragraph E of article XXI or whenever a member is unwilling to accept an amendment to this Statute, it may withdraw from the Agency by notice in writing to that effect given to the depositary Government referred to in paragraph C of article XXI, which shall promptly inform the Board of Governors and all members. E. Withdrawal by a member from the Agency shall not affect its contractual obligations entered into pursuant to article XI or its budgetary obligations for the year in which it withdraws. Article XIX. A. A member of the Agency which is in arrears in the payment of its financial contributions to the Agency shall have no vote in the Agency if the amount of its arrears equals or exceeds the amount of the contributions due from it for the preceding two years. The General Conference may, nevertheless, permit such a member to vote if it is satisfied that the failure to pay is due to conditions beyond the control of the member.

Specialized Agency	*Provisions for Membership*	*Provisions for Withdrawal or Arrears*
		B. A member which has persistently violated the provisions of this Statute or of any agreement entered into by it pursuant to this Statute may be suspended from the exercise of the privileges and rights of membership by the General Conference acting by a two- thirds majority of the members present and voting upon recommendation by the Board of Governors.

Source: CRS; various U.N. specialized agency conventions, statutes, or constitutions.

Note: The United States is currently withholding funding to UNESCO; however, it remains a member of the organization. An asterisk* denotes U.S. membership.

End Notes

[1] This report refers to "Palestine" in the context of the U.N. system. According to U.N. General Assembly resolution 43/167, adopted December 15, 1988, "the designation 'Palestine' should be used in place of the designation 'Palestine Liberation Organization' in the United Nations system."

[2] For a full list of U.N. specialized agencies, see "U.N. Specialized Agencies" text box below.

[3] For more information, see CRS Report RL33848, *United Nations Reform: Background and Issues for Congress*, by Luisa Blanchfield, and CRS Report RL33611, *United Nations System Funding: Congressional Issues*, by Marjorie Ann Browne.

[4] The U.N. Charter was adopted and opened for signature at the San Francisco Conference in June 1945. Participants in the Conference were those countries that had declared war on Germany and Japan and had subscribed by January 1, 1942 to the United Nations Declaration. For more information, see http://www.un.org/en/aboutun/history/sanfrancisco_conference.shtml. A copy of the U.N. Charter is available at http://www.un.org/en/documents/charter/.

[5] Some details of the process for U.N. membership are outlined in the U.N. General Assembly's and U.N. Security Council's rules of procedures. For more detailed information, see the "Paths to U.N. Membership: Criteria and Process" section.

[6] "Membership and Representation of States," in *A Concise Encyclopedia of the United Nations*, ed. Helmut Volger (The Hague: Kluwer Law International, 2002), pp. 369-371.

[7] *The Montevideo Convention on the Rights and Duties of States.* The Convention's definition of statehood is widely cited by international law experts. The treaty was adopted at the International Conference of American States in Montevideo, Uruguay on December 26, 1933. The United States ratified the Convention on June 29, 1934. For further discussion of statehood issues, see Thomas D. Grant, "Defining Statehood: The Montevideo Convention and its Discontents," *Columbia Journal of Transnational Law*, vol. 37 (1998), pp. 403-453. Also see, James R. Crawford, *The Creation of States in International Law* (London: Oxford University Press, 2007).

[8] United Nations website, "About U.N. Membership," at http://www.un.org/en/members/about.shtml.

[9] Connie L. McNeely, *Constructing the Nation State - International Organization and Prescriptive Action* (Westport, CT: Greenwood Press, 1995).

[10] Parts of this section are drawn from *The Charter of the United Nations: A Commentary*, ed. Bruno Simma et al., 3rd ed., vol. I (London: Oxford University Press, 2012) pp. 185-187 (hereinafter referred to by its title). For additional reading, see Thomas D. Grant, *Admission to the United Nations: Charter Article 4 and the Rise of Universal Organization* (The Netherlands: Martinus Nijhoff, 2009); and John Dugard, *Recognition and the United Nations* (Cambridge: Grotius Publishing, 1987).

[11] *The Charter of the United Nations: A Commentary,* p. 185.

[12] Ibid., p. 186.

[13] *The Montevideo Convention on the Rights and Duties of States*, December 26, 1933.

[14] Article 1, paragraph 1, of the U.N. Charter states that the purpose of the United Nations is to, among other things, "maintain international peace and security."

[15] The declaration would include the principles set forth in Article 2 of the Charter that the obligation to settle international disputes by peaceful means and to refrain from the threat or use of force against the territorial integrity or political independence of any state.

[16] These indicators are drawn from *The Charter of the United Nations: A Commentary*, pp. 346-350.

[17] In accordance with Rule 59 of the *Provisional Rules of Procedure of the Security Council*, "Unless the Security Council decides otherwise, the application shall be referred by the President to a committee of the Security Council upon which each member of the Security Council shall be represented. The committee shall examine any application referred to it and report its conclusions thereon to the Council not less than thirty-five days in advance of a regular session of the General Assembly or, if a special session of the General Assembly is called, not less than fourteen days in advance of such session."

[18] Rule 60 of the *Provisional Rules of Procedure of the Security Council.*

[19] Ibid.

[20] Rule 138 of the *Rules of Procedure of the General Assembly.*

[21] U.N. General Assembly Resolution 296 J (IV), November 22, 1949.

[22] International Court of Justice, Advisory Opinion, Competence of the General Assembly for the Admission of a State to the United Nations (1950). For more information, see *Yearbook of the United Nations, 1950* (NY: Columbia University Press, 1951), pp. 409-413.

[23] For further discussion of Article 5, see *The Charter of the United Nations: A Commentary,* pp. 365-373.

[24] Under Article 27 of the U.N. Charter, non-procedural decisions by Security Council members shall be made by an affirmative vote of nine members, including the P-5.

[25] Article 19 addresses financial arrears. It states, "A member of the United Nations which is in arrears in the payment of its financial contributions to the Organization shall have no vote in the General Assembly if the amount of its arrears equals or exceeds the amount of the contributions due from it for the preceding two full years. The General Assembly may, nevertheless, permit such a Member to vote if it is satisfied that the failure to pay is due to conditions beyond the control of the Member."

[26] The General Assembly's Credentials Committee examines and accepts the credentials of delegations to the Assembly, ensuring that they have been signed by either Head of State or Government or by the Minister of Foreign Affairs for the member state. In this way, credentials of the majority of U.N. members have been routinely accepted for participation in each General Assembly session since it first convened in 1946. However, some credentials have been challenged—usually to change the political status of the government involved or to promote the foreign policies of the challenging country. For more information, see U.S. Congress, Senate Committee on Foreign Relations, *Credentials Considerations in the United Nations General Assembly: The Process and Its Role*, committee print, prepared by Congressional Research Service, 98th Cong., 1st sess., December 1983, S. Prt. 98-143 (Washington: GPO, 1983), and "Credentials Committee," at http://www.un.org/en/ga/credentials/credentials.shtml.

[27] International organizations and institutions may also be invited to observe the work of the General Assembly. For a full list of these observers, see http://www.un.org/en/members/intergovorg.shtml.

[28] According to the United Nations, the IAEA is not a specialized agency in the strict legal sense; however, for all intents and purposes it operates like one. It reports to the General Assembly and, when appropriate, to the Security Council. Like U.N. specialized agencies, it also reports to the U.N. Economic and Social Council. See *The U.N. System* on the U.N. Chief Executive Board's website, at http://www.unsceb.org/content/un-system.

[29] Each organization has a "specialized agency" arrangement or agreement with the United Nations under Article 57 of the U.N. Charter, and reports to the U.N. Economic and Social Council.

[30] "IFM Quotas Fact Sheet," International Monetary Fund," March 25, 2014, at http://www.imf.org/external/np/exr/ facts/quotas.htm.

[31] For example, Article 8 of the WHO's constitution states, "Territories or groups of territories which are not responsible for the conduct of their international relations may be admitted as Associate Members by the Health Assembly upon application made on behalf of such territory or group of territories by the Member or other authority having responsibility for their international relations." Puerto Rico and Tokelau are associate members of the WHO.

[32] This section focuses on the process and status of Palestinian membership efforts in the context of the United Nations and U.N. system. For information on Palestinian, U.S., and regional perspectives on this issue, see CRS Report RL34074, *The Palestinians: Background and U.S. Relations*, by Jim Zanotti. A more detailed analysis of UNESCO is available in CRS Report R42999, *The United Nations Educational, Scientific, and Cultural Organization (UNESCO)*, by Luisa Blanchfield and Marjorie Ann Browne.

[33] See U.N. document, S/2011/705, November 11, 2011. For more information on Council process, see "Role of the Security Council" section.

[34] U.N. document, A/RES/67/19, adopted November 29, 2012.

[35] These include participation in General Assembly debates, the right of reply, the right to raise points of order, the ability to co-sponsor draft resolutions and decisions related to proceedings on Palestinian and Middle East issues, and the right to maintain permanent offices at U.N. headquarters.

[36] However, in November 2013, the "State of Palestine" participated in the balloting for a judge for the International Tribunal for the Former Yugoslavia. Article 13, Section 2(d) of the Statute for the Tribunal (Annex to U.N. Doc. S/25704, adopted pursuant to U.N. Security Council Resolution 827 (1993), as subsequently amended) includes "non-Member States maintaining permanent observer missions at United Nations Headquarters" in the election of the tribunal's judges.

[37] For more information, see PLO Negotiations Affairs Department, "Q&A: Palestine's Accession to International Treaties," April 2, 2014, at http://nad-plo.org/userfiles/file/fact%20sheets/Q&A%20Accession.pdf.

[38] This section was written by Matthew C. Weed, CRS Analyst in Foreign Policy Legislation.

[39] Article 12(3).

[40] Based on the date of entry into force of the Rome Statute, the ICC can only exercise jurisdiction over crimes committed on or after July 1, 2002.

[41] The Assembly of States Parties (ASP) is made up of representatives of the parties to the Rome Statute and carries out oversight and certain administrative functions.

[42] International Criminal Court, Office of the Prosecutor, *Report on Preliminary Examination Activities, 2013*, November 2013, pp. 53-54.

[43] See, for instance, H.Con.Res. 293 [107th], "Expressing the sense of the Congress that the United Nations should suspend the membership of any state identified as a sponsor of terrorism by the Department of State."

[44] Section 8 of the United Nations Participation Act of 1945 (P.L. 79-264; 22 U.S.C. 287e), authorizes appropriations to the Department of State for U.S. participation in the United Nations.

[45] Current withholdings are approximately $80 million over three fiscal years (FY2012 through FY2014), or 22% of the UNESCO regular budget.

[46] See, for instance, Transcript, Hearing on President Obama's Proposed Fiscal 2015 Budget Request for the State Department before the House Committee on Foreign Affairs, March 13, 2014.

[47] The United States opposed UNESCO member states' decision to admit Palestine as a member—arguing that Palestinian statehood can only be realized through direct negotiations between Israel and the Palestinians, and not through membership in international organizations. For more information on Palestinian membership in UNESCO and U.S. policy, see CRS Report R42999, *The United Nations Educational, Scientific, and Cultural Organization (UNESCO)*, by Luisa Blanchfield and Marjorie Ann Browne.

[48] See, for example, H.R. 1337, Palestinian Accountability Act, introduced on March 21, 2013, and referred to the Committee on Foreign Affairs (HFAC); and Title III of S. 1313, The United Nations, Transparency, Accountability and Reform Act of 2013, introduced on September 19, 2013 and referred to the Senate Committee on Foreign Relations (also see Title IV of the House version of this bill, H.R. 3155).

[49] Taiwan is not a member of the United Nations; however, it has sought to participate or obtain membership in various U.N.-related bodies. For more information, see CRS Report R41952, *U.S.-Taiwan Relationship: Overview of Policy Issues*, by Shirley A. Kan and Wayne M. Morrison. Regarding legislation, see, H.R. 419, Taiwan Policy Act of 2013, introduced January 25, 2013, and referred to HFAC; and H.Con.Res. 55, Expressing the Sense of Congress that Taiwan and its 23,000,000 people deserve membership in the United Nations, introduced on September 16, 2013 and referred to HFAC.

In: Membership in the United Nations ... ISBN: 978-1-63321-971-7
Editor: Elizabeth Saunders

Chapter 2

THE UNITED NATIONS EDUCATIONAL, SCIENTIFIC, AND CULTURAL ORGANIZATION (UNESCO)*

Luisa Blanchfield and Marjorie Ann Browne

SUMMARY

Recent international events have renewed congressional interest in the United Nations Educational, Scientific and Cultural Organization (UNESCO). UNESCO is a specialized agency of the U.N. system that promotes collaboration among its member countries in the fields of education, natural sciences, social and human sciences, culture, and communications and information. With an annual budget of approximately $326 million, it supports nearly 2,000 staff members working at its headquarters in Paris and 65 field offices and institutes worldwide. UNESCO activities are funded through a combination of assessed contributions by member states to its regular budget, and voluntary contributions by member states and organizations.

---

* This is an edited, reformatted and augmented version of a Congressional Research Service publication, No. R42999, dated January 23, 2014.

U.S. Policy

The United States is a member of UNESCO and generally supports the organization's objectives. Over the years, however, some U.S. policy makers—particularly some Members of Congress— have expressed strong concern with UNESCO's politicization and, as some have alleged, lack of budget discipline and anti-democratic leanings. These concerns led to the United States' decision to withdraw from UNESCO in 1984. Since the United States rejoined the organization in 2003, Congress has demonstrated support for UNESCO—appropriating between $73 million and $84 million in assessed contributions per fiscal year, or about 22% of UNESCO's annual regular budget. It has maintained an ongoing interest in ensuring that UNESCO runs as efficiently and effectively as possible, and that its policies and programs are in line with U.S. priorities.

Palestinian Membership: U.S. Financial Withholding, FY2012–FY2014

Since late 2011, UNESCO has received significant U.S. and international attention resulting from member states' decision to admit "Palestine" as a member. The Obama Administration and many Members of Congress vehemently opposed this action, maintaining that Palestinian statehood can only be realized through direct negotiation between Israelis and Palestinians rather than through membership in U.N. entities. Subsequently, the United States withheld approximately $80 million in FY2012 through FY2014 funding to UNESCO. Two laws enacted in the 1990s prohibit funding to U.N. entities that admit the PLO (Palestine Liberation Organization) as a member (P.L. 101-246), or grant full membership as a state to any organization or group that does not have the internationally recognized attributes of statehood (P.L. 103-236). The Obama Administration asked Congress to enact legislation to waive the aforementioned restrictions.

In November 2013, as a result of the financial withholding, the United States lost its vote in the UNESCO General Conference (GC), the organization's main decision-making body. The Obama Administration has emphasized that the United States remains a member of the organization and that it intends to "continue its engagement with UNESCO in every possible way."

Reform

Since UNESCO's establishment, member states have sought to improve the organization's effectiveness through reform. Many observers, including the United States, agree that UNESCO has successfully implemented various reforms, particularly during the time between the United States' decision to withdraw from the organization in 1984 and its return in 2003. At the same time, many experts argue that the organization needs additional reform. Weaknesses in UNESCO's structure and culture, they contend, hinder its ability to fulfill its mission.

A 2010 Independent External Evaluation report commissioned by member states recommends changing some of UNESCO's management processes, enhancing UNESCO's field presence, and strengthening the organization's governance mechanisms. Ultimately, the full impact of these and other reform efforts is unclear. Their success—and the success of any future reforms—will likely depend on how effectively both UNESCO and its members follow through on implementation.

Issues for the 113th Congress

The recent controversy over Palestinian membership and loss of the United States' vote in the General Conference—coupled with broad concerns about spending levels in light of the recent economic downturn—have prompted some policy makers and observers to review the U.S. relationship with UNESCO. Examples of issues being considered are described below.

- **Effect on U.S. priorities.** Some experts and policy makers worry that the U.S. financial withholding and loss of voting rights in the GC have negatively impacted programs and activities that the United States views as priorities— including U.S. World Heritage sites, Holocaust education programs, tsunami early warning systems, and educational programs for women and girls.
- **The impact of the U.S. financial withholding on UNESCO's activities.** Many experts agree that the U.S. withholding has adversely affected the scope and effectiveness of UNESCO's programs. There are disagreements, however, regarding the extent of this impact. The long-term implications of the withholding remain to be seen and are largely dependent on how long the United States withholds funds and what fiscal actions, if any, UNESCO continues to take in response to the funding decrease.

- **The effectiveness of the U.S. withholding.** Some policy makers argue that the legislative restrictions prompting the U.S. withholding are no longer relevant or effective and should be waived. Others, however, contend that waiving the legislation would undermine U.S. credibility and provide a "green light" for Palestine to apply for membership in entities across the U.N. system.
- **UNESCO's role in U.S. foreign policy.** Some critics of UNESCO maintain that its activities do not reflect U.S. foreign policy interests. Supporters contend that the organization plays a key role in global issues that the United States views as strategic priorities, particularly education and science.
- **Challenges to UNESCO reform.** A significant obstacle to UNESCO reform is governments' differing views on the organization's role in the global multilateral framework. Moreover, each UNESCO member state has its own foreign policy priorities, political agenda, and perceptions of how the organization should work. These differences can lead to disagreements on budgeting, programming and, as most recently demonstrated, membership.

INTRODUCTION

During the past several decades, the United States has had a mixed relationship with the United Nations Educational, Scientific and Cultural Organization (UNESCO). Most recently, decisions by some UNESCO member states have led to increased congressional interest in U.S. funding of and participation in the organization. Established in 1946 in the aftermath of World War II, UNESCO aims to contribute to peace and security by promoting collaboration among member states in the fields of education, science, and culture. The organization, which has a specialized agency relationship with the United Nations, is headquartered in Paris, France, and composed of 195 member states. With an annual budget of about $326 million, its programs and activities encompass a wide array of issues, including literacy, media and Internet freedom, ocean management, and environmental and cultural preservation, among others.

The United States played a key role in UNESCO's establishment and has generally supported the overall objectives of the organization. At the same time, U.S. policy makers—particularly some Members of Congress—have expressed concern with UNESCO's apparent politicization, lack of budget discipline, and perceived leanings toward anti-democratic countries. These concerns led to the United States' withdrawal from UNESCO in 1984. Since the United States rejoined the organization in 2003, Congress has demonstrated support for UNESCO—appropriating about $618.6 million in regular budget contributions and $9.5 million in voluntary contributions from FY2004 through FY2011.

In October 2011, UNESCO garnered significant attention from U.S. policy makers when a majority of member countries decided to admit "Palestine" as a member.[1] (The decision to pursue UNESCO membership was part of a broader, ongoing effort by Palestine Liberation Organization Chairman and Palestinian Authority President Mahmoud Abbas to achieve membership or nonmember observer state status in various U.N. bodies as a means for achieving recognition of Palestinian statehood.)[2] As a result of this decision, the United States withheld its contributions to UNESCO in accordance with two laws enacted in the 1990s that prohibit funding to U.N. entities that admit the Palestine Liberation Organization (PLO) as a member (P.L. 101-246), or grant full membership as a state to any organization or group that does not have the internationally recognized attributes of statehood (P.L. 103-236). From FY2012 through FY2014, the United States withheld nearly $80 million per year, or 22% of the UNESCO annual regular budget.

The Obama Administration actively opposes Palestinian membership in UNESCO. It argues that Palestinian statehood can only be realized through direct negotiation between Israel and the Palestinians, and not through membership in international organizations. At the same time, the Administration maintains that U.S. participation in UNESCO is in the interest of the United States and that the government should continue to fund and participate in the organization. In his FY2013 and FY2014 budget proposals, President Obama requested nearly $80 million in assessed contributions for UNESCO, and stated that the Administration intended to work with Congress to "waive" the funding restrictions. In both FY2013 and FY2014, Congress did not enact a waiver. Critics argued that waiving the laws would undermine U.S. credibility and encourage the Palestinians to continue to pursue membership in other U.N. entities.

As the debate over U.S. funding of and participation in UNESCO moves forward, Congress may consider a number of issues, including UNESCO's role, if any, in U.S. foreign policy, as well as the organization's overall effectiveness and reform efforts. It may also consider the long- and short-term implications, both positive and negative, of withholding funding to UNESCO. More broadly, policy makers might consider the efficacy of laws restricting funding for U.N. entities that admit Palestine as a member. A particularly pressing question moving forward is how, if at all, the United States will engage with UNESCO given its ongoing financial withholding and loss of voting rights in the General Conference.

ORGANIZATION AND STRUCTURE

UNESCO programs and activities encompass five sectors—education, natural sciences, social and human sciences, culture, and communication and information. The organization sponsors international exchanges and meetings in science, education, and other fields; promotes the free flow of ideas, including media freedom; encourages the conservation of books, monuments, and works of art; and assists member states in developing educational, scientific, and cultural programs. It also provides a mechanism for the drafting, adoption, and review of several international conventions and commissions, including the Convention concerning the Protection of the World Cultural and Natural Heritage (often referred to as the World Heritage Convention), the Intergovernmental Oceanographic Commission (IOC), and the Convention against Discrimination in Education.[4]

Role in the U.N. System[3]

UNESCO is a specialized agency of the U.N. system. Articles 57 and 63 of the U.N. Charter state that specialized agencies are autonomous intergovernmental organizations *"having wide international responsibilities I ... j in economic, social, cultural, educational, health and related fields."*

Like other specialized agencies, UNESCO has its own constitution, governance structure, budget, and programs. It regularly collaborates with the United Nations and other specialized agencies at the intergovernmental level through regular reporting to and interaction with the United Nations. Examples of other U.N. specialized agencies include the World Health Organization, International Labor Organization, and Food and Agriculture Organization.

More than 2,000 personnel from 170 countries work for UNESCO; approximately 850 staff work in the organization's 65 field offices and institutes worldwide.[5] UNESCO's governing structure consists of three key mechanisms, described as follows.

- The **General Conference** (GC), composed of representatives from all member countries, is UNESCO's primary decision-making body. It meets every two years to determine the organization's policies, programs, and budget. With a few exceptions, GC decisions on important questions are made by consensus; consequently, approved resolutions are often not very specific, even those addressing budgetary issues.
- The **Executive Board**, composed of 58 member state representatives, meets twice a year and is responsible for implementing the program adopted by the GC. Members are elected to the Board by the GC for a four-year term. The United States is currently a member of the Board; its term will expire in 2015.
- The **Director-General** (DG), currently Irina Bokova of Bulgaria, heads the UNESCO Secretariat. The DG is appointed to a four-year term by the GC on the recommendation of the Executive Board. She is charged with preparing the UNESCO program and budget, making proposals to the GC, creating the organizational structures of the Secretariat, and appointing staff. The DG can also play a key role in negotiations regarding budgets, resolutions, and programs.

The Executive Board and GC include various committees composed of member countries that consider issues related to the functioning of the organization or specific issues related to education, science, or culture.[6]

UNESCO maintains relationships with non-governmental organizations (NGOs), foundations, the private sector, and intergovernmental organizations (IGOs). More than 350 NGOs and 20 foundations have an official relationship with UNESCO, and many more work with the organization on specific activities and programs at the local, national, and international level. UNESCO also works with several hundred private companies and organizations through traditional philanthropic and sponsorship relationships, as well as strategic partnerships developed through shared resources and expertise. In addition, it collaborates with more than 80 IGOs, including the European Union (EU) and various multilateral development banks, on specific programs and projects through formal agreements or ad hoc arrangements.[7] UNESCO also partners and coordinates with other parts of the U.N. system through various system-wide coordination mechanisms and memoranda of understanding with other U.N. entities.[8]

UNESCO's relationships with other organizations are strengthened by National Commissions established by member governments in their respective countries. The commissions aim to provide links among UNESCO and NGOs, the private sector, local and national governments, and the public in each country. Commission members, who are appointed by governments, provide insight on UNESCO programs, and help implement training programs, studies, public awareness campaigns, and media outreach. There are currently 199 National Commissions worldwide, including one in the United States.[9]

FUNDING AND BUDGET

UNESCO activities are funded through a combination of assessed contributions by member states to the regular budget; voluntary contributions by member states, organizations, and others to special programs; and funds provided by partners such as other U.N. entities, NGOs, and the private sector. The U.S. share of UNESCO's regular budget is 22%, the largest among contributing members. Four countries—the United States, Japan (assessed at 15%), Germany (8%), and France (6%)—account for more than 50% of the assessed budget.

UNESCO's recent budget and cash flow have been significantly affected by member countries' October 2011 decision to admit Palestine as a member.[10] As a result of Palestine's membership, the United States began to withhold its contributions to UNESCO in FY2012. Two laws enacted in the 1990s prohibit funding to U.N. entities that admit the PLO as a member (P.L. 101-246), or that grant full membership as a state to any organization or group that does not have the internationally recognized attributes of statehood (P.L. 103-236).[11]

The UNESCO budget for 2010-2011 was $653 million, or about $326.5 million annually. The start of U.S. suspension of contributions, however, left UNESCO with immediate shortfall of $72 million by the end of 2011. Funding for the 2012-2013 budget, which was originally $653 million, was also affected by the U.S. withholding. It was decreased to $465 million, or about $232.5 annually—representing a $188 million (or 29%) funding reduction. To cover these budget shortfalls, Director-General Bokova has introduced a number of initiatives and funding reductions, including:

- launching an Emergency Multi-Donor Fund for UNESCO Priority Programs and Reform Initiatives, which accepts financial contributions from countries, institutions, and individuals to cover the gaps left by U.S. withholdings (as of late 2013, the Fund had received $75.1 million);[12]
- cutting staff mission travel costs by 73%, reducing consultant costs by 70%, and decreasing furniture and equipment costs by 64%; and
- abolishing over 40 staff posts (of the 1,854 staff posts funded under the regular budget, 311 remained vacant as of December 2012, the last date for which information is available).[13]

In a September 2013 address to the Executive Board, DG Bokova stated that because of the aforementioned actions, UNESCO has "sustained the impact of the financial crisis [of the U.S. withholding]" and "balanced the books."[14] At the same time, she argued that the new fiscal environment does not provide UNESCO with the resources to fulfill its broad mission. Bokova has also stated that fundraising efforts such as the Multi-Donor Fund are not long-term solutions to the funding gaps.[15]

EFFECTIVENESS AND REFORM

Many U.S. policy makers generally support UNESCO's aim of promoting international collaboration in the fields of education, science, and communication. At the same time, some are concerned that the organization is not fulfilling its mission as efficiently or effectively as possible. This section describes concerns expressed by UNESCO critics, including some Members of Congress, regarding the organization's alleged politicization and organizational and cultural weaknesses. It also describes UNESCO's efforts to address some of these issues through internal evaluations and reform.

Politicization Concerns

One criticism that UNESCO faces, perhaps more than most U.N. specialized agencies, is politicization among its membership. Observers contend that in the General Conference and Executive Board, governments often focus on subjects unrelated to UNESCO's mission rather than issues such as education, science, or improving the organization's effectiveness.

Most recently, some U.S. policy makers have raised questions and concerns regarding (1) UNESCO's decision to admit Palestine as a member, and (2) the composition of UNESCO's committees.

Palestinian Membership

In October 2011, UNESCO generated significant controversy both domestically and internationally when its General Conference adopted a resolution admitting Palestine as a member. (See **text box** for a chronology of Palestinian membership actions.) Some U.S. officials and observers viewed this as a political decision that reflected member states' long-standing and disproportionate focus on Israel within UNESCO and the U.N. system. Palestinian efforts to achieve UNESCO membership were part of broader efforts by PLO Chairman and Palestinian Authority President Mahmoud Abbas to achieve international recognition for Palestinian statehood. On November 29, 2012, the U.N. General Assembly voted to change Palestine's observer status from "observer entity," to "non-member observer state" by a vote of 138 in favor, 9 against (including the United States), and 41 abstaining.[16]

"Palestine" and UNESCO Membership

Under the UNESCO Constitution, membership in the United Nations can qualify a state for membership in UNESCO. However, states that are not members of the United Nations—such as "Palestine"—may be admitted to UNESCO on the recommendation of the Executive Board, followed by a two-thirds majority vote in the General Conference.

Chronology

April 27, 1989—The PLO, following its 1988 declaration of Palestinian statehood, submitted a request to the Executive Board asking that it be admitted as a UNESCO member. Up to October 2011, the Board and the GC deferred consideration of the application and referred the agenda item to subsequent sessions of the Executive Board and GC.

October 5, 2011—The Executive Board, by a roll call vote of 40 in favor, 4 against, and 14 abstaining, decided to recommend that the General Conference admit Palestine as a UNESCO member.

October 31, 2011—The UNESCO GC, by a vote of 107 in favor, 14 against, and 52 abstaining, adopted a resolution admitting Palestine as a member.

November 23, 2011—Effective date of Palestinian membership in UNESCO per receipt of Palestine's notification of its signature and ratification of the UNESCO Constitution.

Committee Composition

Some U.S. policy makers have raised concerns regarding the membership of UNESCO committees. Specifically, the Executive Board's Committee on Conventions and Recommendations (CR), which considers the periodic reports of members on the implementation of UNESCO recommendations and conventions, has been criticized by some governments, including the United States, for Syria's membership. Many are concerned that human rights abuses by the Syrian government impact the credibility of the CR committee, which is charged with, among other things, assessing countries' compliance with conventions that address human rights issues. In January 2012, the United States and other like-minded countries led an unsuccessful diplomatic effort to remove Syria from the committee. U.S. Permanent Ambassador to UNESCO David Killion stated, "We should not allow the Syrian regime to stand as a judge of other countries' human rights record while it systematically violates the human rights of its citizens."[17] CR committee members, who are elected by and from within the Executive Board, serve two-year terms. Syria remains a member of the CR committee, and its term is set to expire in late 2014.

Organizational Culture and Priorities

Some experts contend that UNESCO's organizational structure and culture hinder its ability to fulfill its objectives. For example, many are concerned that UNESCO's hiring and promotion practices have little transparency and lack consistent implementation. Critics maintain that hiring practices appear to favor geographic representation and gender balance with too little consideration of merit. They emphasize that issues such as employee progress and managerial accountability should be addressed to "avoid [staff] frustration" that may affect UNESCO's effectiveness.[18] In addition, critics assert that UNESCO's governance structure is "unwieldy," with weeks-long meetings that encourage long debates focused on administrative rather than substantive matters and time-consuming reporting requirements for Secretariat staff.[19] Some have also expressed concern with what has been called an "inward-oriented" and risk-averse culture, as well as lack of collaboration and communication within and among UNESCO sectors.[20]

Additionally, a number of experts have emphasized the apparent imbalance between UNESCO's administrative and programmatic costs. For example, prior to the adjustment for the U.S. financial withholding, the 2012-2013 biennium budget was $653 million (about $327 million per year); $57.7 million (about 17%) of that yearly budget was allocated for the education sector, with staff costs accounting for nearly $32 million, leaving about $25 million for actual education activities and programs.[21] This problem has been exacerbated over the years as UNESCO's real budget has decreased but staffing costs have increased, which has reduced available funding for UNESCO programs.[22]

2010 Independent External Evaluation Report Findings

Some of the aforementioned concerns were reflected in an August 2010 UNESCO Independent External Evaluation (IEE) report commissioned by the Executive Board and GC.[23] The report found that while UNESCO is valued and its achievements are recognized by many, the organization is "unevenly" meeting its mandate. Evaluators noted that the organization's broad mission is "permissive," meaning that UNESCO could claim to play a role in any worldwide issue—leading to instances of programmatic incoherence and general lack of focus. Moreover, while UNESCO has sought to concentrate or improve the focus in larger program areas and across sectors, these efforts have been undermined by "weak incentives for collaboration, sectoral budget systems, too many priorities and cross-cutting objectives, and lack of consensus in governing bodies and in the [UNESCO] Secretariat."[24]

Another issue raised in the IEE report was the effectiveness of UNESCO's field presence. The report stated that UNESCO field offices are "over-extended, often under-resourced, and poorly staffed," and that they might benefit from "a smaller number of more capable and well-resourced multi-skilled ... regional and subregional bureaus."[25] In addition, the report highlighted the challenge of measuring the effectiveness of UNESCO activities, noting that evidence of UNESCO's impact tends to be largely anecdotal. It found that while UNESCO has invested in results-based management, the "evaluation culture" in the organization is weak, noting that recommendations stemming from evaluations and assessment were not fully implemented. At the same time, the report acknowledged that the broad and often intangible nature of UNESCO's mission makes it difficult to measure the organization's impact. It also emphasizes that evaluations and assessments may be complex and costly.

To address these and other issues, the report recommended five broad "strategic directions" for UNESCO:

- *Focus*—improving the organization's focus to address challenges consistent with its mandate;
- *Field*—positioning UNESCO closer to the field to be closer to country needs, resources, and partners;
- *United Nations*—strengthening participation in the U.N. system;
- *Governance*—strengthening governance mechanisms; and
- *Partnership*—developing a partnership strategy that improves its relationship with civil society and the private sector.

Recent Reform Activities

Over the years, UNESCO member states have sought to improve the organization's effectiveness through a range of reform efforts.[26] Many observers, including some in the United States, agree that UNESCO has successfully implemented various reforms, particularly during the time between the United States' decision to withdraw from the organization in 1984 and its return in 2003.[27] Nevertheless, many experts and policy makers in the international community and the United States maintain that additional changes are needed to ensure that UNESCO is successful in achieving its mission.

The most recent wave of reform activities is driven in part by the strategic directions recommended in the aforementioned Independent External Evaluation report.[28] After the report was published, the Executive Board and GC agreed to 87 "action points," which are in various states of implementation.[29] UNESCO reports that as of September 2013, 70 of 87 points were completed.[30] Completed activities include adjusting the scope, actions, and expected results in future budgeting and programming cycles; reviewing UNESCO's partnership agreements with other U.N. entities and identifying areas for future collaboration; and implementing the first phase of a decentralization strategy that works to reform field networks in Africa and Arab states by clarifying the roles, responsibilities, and functions of various UNESCO field offices.[31]

Separate from IEE-related reforms, member states agreed to a human resources management strategy for 2011 through 2016 that focuses on

- improving talent management (attracting and retaining talented people committed to the values of the organization);
- enhancing staff capacity (developing efficient and effective staff capabilities); and
- creating an enabling work environment (by providing the necessary internal conditions to support staff commitment and motivation).[32]

UNESCO also continues to participate in broader U.N. reform-related efforts, including systemwide coherence efforts such as the "Delivering as One" pilot initiative established in eight countries in 2006 to improve coordination and cooperation among U.N. Country Team members.

The full impact of these recent reform efforts is still unclear. Their overall success—and the success of any future reform efforts—will largely depend on how effectively both UNESCO and its member countries follow through on implementation.[33]

U.S. Policy

The United States was one of the original members of UNESCO and has generally supported the organization's overall objectives.[34] At the same time, U.S. policy makers, including some Members of Congress, have been critical of the organization, leading to the United States' nearly 20-year withdrawal in 1984, followed by its subsequent decision to rejoin in 2003. (See **text box** for more details.)

U.S.Withdrawal: 1984-2003

In December 1983, the Secretary of State notified then-Director-General of UNESCO, Amadou-Mahter M'Bow of Senegal, that the United States would be terminating its membership in the organization, effective in December 1984. Three key concerns influenced the U.S. decision. The first was UNESCO's apparent politicization, which included GC actions that (1) targeted Israel, and (2) shifted the definition of human rights from the western concept of individual rights to that of "collective peoples' rights."

The second concern was the organization's hostility toward the basic institutions of a free society through its support of activities in international communications, which many western countries viewed as a threat to freedom of the press. Finally, many were concerned with UNESCO's lack of adherence to the U.S.-proposed "zero net program growth" for all international entities, as well as with apparent mismanagement problems and high overhead costs under DG M'Bow. In September 2002, President George W. Bush, in a speech before the U.N. General Assembly, announced that the United States would rejoin UNESCO. The President stated that the organization had been reformed and that the United States would "participate fully in UNESCO's mission to advance human rights, tolerance, and learning."[35] The United States officially rejoined in October 2003.

The United States engages with UNESCO through the U.S. Mission to UNESCO, which is located in Paris, France, and headed by a U.S. Permanent Representative. Mission staff, along with temporary staff from U.S. agencies and departments, work with other national delegations and subject-area experts to further U.S. policy priorities in UNESCO.[36] Such priorities include combating illiteracy, improving water resource management, monitoring climate change, enhancing tsunami early warning systems, preserving world heritage sites, and promoting free media worldwide.[37] The United States also engages with and supports the U.S. National Commission to UNESCO, which includes experts from non-governmental, federal, state, and local government sectors.[38]

Response to Palestinian Membership

The United States is currently withholding its voluntary and assessed contributions to UNESCO as a result of the General Conference's October 2011 decision to admit Palestine as a member. As previously mentioned, two provisions in U.S. law prohibit funding to U.N. entities that admit the PLO as a member or grant full membership as a state to any organization or group that does not have the internationally recognized attributes of statehood:[39]

- **Section 410 of the Foreign Relations Authorization Act, Fiscal Years 1994 and 1995 (P.L. 103-236)** states that the United States shall not make contributions to "any affiliated organization of the

United Nations which grants full membership as a state to any organization or group that does not have the internationally recognized attributes of statehood"; and

- **Section 414 of the Foreign Relations Authorization Act, Fiscal Years 1990 and 1991 (P.L. 101-246)** states, "No funds authorized to be appropriated by this Act or any other Act shall be available for the United Nations or any specialized agencies thereof which accords the Palestine Liberation Organization the same standing as member states."

The United States voted against the Executive Board and GC actions that led to Palestine's admission as a UNESCO member. Obama Administration officials stated that the GC's decision was "regrettable and premature," and emphasized that the United States "remains steadfast in its support for the establishment of an independent and sovereign Palestinian state.... [S]uch a state can only be realized through direct negotiations between the Israelis and Palestinians."[40] At the same time, officials expressed deep commitment to the organization and pledged to find ways to support and strengthen its work. The State Department reports that since the U.S. withholding, the U.S. Mission to UNESCO has shifted its focus toward emphasizing the value of U.S. engagement in the organization and maintaining U.S. influence.[41]

In November 2013, the United States lost its vote in the UNESCO General Conference (GC) under Article IV of the organization's constitution.[42] Article IV states that a member state shall have no vote in the GC if the total amount of contributions due exceeds the total amount of contributions payable by it for the current year and the immediately preceding calendar year. The United States owed assessments for two consecutive calendar years (2011 and 2012) in late 2013, and thus was deemed ineligible to vote in the GC.

In statements made after the United States lost its vote, Obama Administration officials emphasized that the United States would remain a member of the UNESCO. They recognized the organization as a "critical partner," and noted that the United States intends to "continue its engagement with UNESCO in every possible way."[43] The Administration further emphasized that the United States would attend meetings, participate in debates, and maintain its seat on, and vote as an elected member of, the UNESCO Executive Board.[44]

U.S. Contributions, FY2004-FY2014

As a member of UNESCO, the United States is assessed to pay 22% of the UNESCO regular budget, or roughly $80 million a year. This contribution is financed from the Contributions to International Organizations (CIO) appropriations account. The United States has also made voluntary contributions to selected UNESCO programs—particularly the Intergovernmental Oceanographic Commission (IOC) and World Heritage Fund—through the International Organizations and Programs (IO&P) account.[45] (Both the accounts are typically funded through the Department of State, Foreign Operations and Related Programs Appropriations Act.)

Table 1. U.S. Contributions to UNESCO: FY2004-FY2014 (in millions of current U.S. dollars)

	2004	2005	2006	2007	2008	2009	2010	2011	2012	2013	2014
Assessed (CIO)	84.14	76.75	70.92	73.48	77.62	75.94	80.92	78.83	0.00a	0.00	0.00
Voluntary (IO&P)	1.89	0.84	0.99	0.99	0.99	1.00	1.00	1.85	0.00	0.00	0.00

Source: CRS calculations, Department of State congressional budget justifications, annual appropriations legislation.

Notes: CIO = Contributions to International Organizations account, IO&P = International Organizations and Programs account.

a. As a result of the financial withholding, the United States paid nothing towards calendar year (CY) 2011 assessments to UNESCO (about $79 million depending on the exchange rates), which would have been paid from FY2012 CIO funds.

As demonstrated in **Table 1**, from FY2004 to FY2011, U.S. assessed contributions to UNESCO ranged between $70 million and $84 million per year. Voluntary contributions fluctuated between $840,000 and $1.89 million during the same time period. The United States withheld funding to UNESCO from FY2012 through FY2014. In both FY2013 and FY2014, the President requested nearly $80 million in UNESCO assessed contributions through the CIO account, and $880,000 in UNESCO International Contributions for Scientific, Educational, and Cultural Activities (ICSECA) voluntary funds through the IO&P account.[46] The President also asked Congress to support legislation that would provide authority to waive the legislative restrictions.[47] To waive or modify such restrictions, Congress could (1) enact stand-alone legislation or (2) amend the existing restrictions. To date, Congress has not enacted a waiver.[48]

ISSUES FOR CONGRESS

The controversy over Palestinian membership and the broader political climate of fiscal austerity may prompt some policy makers to take stock of U.S. participation in and funding of UNESCO. This section discusses selected issues that the 113th Congress may wish to consider.

Effect of Withholding on U.S. Priorities

An area of ongoing concern among some U.S. policy makers is the impact that the U.S. withholding and loss of voting rights in the GC may have on U.S. influence within UNESCO. Specifically, many are concerned that the loss of a U.S. vote in the GC will hinder the United States' ability to shape internal UNESCO management and policies. For example, the United States cannot cast a vote for the Director-General or members of UNESCO subsidiary bodies. It also cannot vote for or against various budget proposals considered by the GC.

Some also worry that the financial withholding has negatively impacted activities that the United States views as priorities—including Holocaust education programs, tsunami early warning systems, educational programs for women and girls, World Heritage sites (see **text box** on next page), and various training and literacy programs in the Middle East. In response, some analysts have noted that UNESCO activities widely viewed as U.S. priorities are funded primarily through voluntary contributions from countries other than the United States. (Literacy programs for Afghan soldiers, for example, are funded by voluntary contributions from Japan.)[49] At the same time, UNESCO supporters emphasize that many of the programs funded by voluntary contributions are managed by entities financed through the UNESCO regular budget. (The literacy program in Afghanistan, for instance, is financed through the Afghanistan Field Office and the International Bureau of Education, both of which are funded through the regular budget.)

Impact of Withholding on UNESCO Programs and Activities

U.S. and international policy makers generally agree that the U.S. withholding has negatively affected the scope and effectiveness of UNESCO's programs and activities. There are disagreements, however, regarding the extent of this impact. For example, some officials and experts, including UNESCO DG Irina Bokova, argue that the funding cut has had a crippling effect on existing activities and impeded the organization's ability to fulfill its mandate.[50] At the same time, some experts note that during the U.S. withdrawal between 1984 and 2003, UNESCO was able to fulfill its mission and implement many of its activities without U.S. financial support.[51] Ultimately, the long-term impact of the U.S. withholding on UNESCO activities remains to be seen, and may depend on

- the fiscal or organizational actions, if any, UNESCO continues to take in response to the sudden funding decrease (for example, further adjustments to the organization's budget and programming in both the short and long-term by the Executive Board, GC, and/or DG);
- the extent to which UNESCO can continue to solicit extrabudgetary contributions from other countries, other international organizations, or the private sector, to cover any budget shortfalls; or
- when, if at all, the United States resumes financial contributions to UNESCO (for example, if the United States withholds UNESCO funding for 4 years, the impact would be far less than if it were to withhold contributions for 10 years).

UNESCO World Heritage Sites in the United States

Background. During the past two decades, some Members of Congress have demonstrated an interest in U.S. participation in the UNESCO Convention Concerning the Protection of the World Cultural and Natural Heritage (known as the World Heritage Convention). Under the Convention, countries agree to protect and preserve natural and cultural sites of exceptional ecological, scientific, or cultural importance through the World Heritage List. Congressional perspectives on the Convention have varied. Some Members of Congress have supported the Convention, while others have expressed concern that UNESCO designation of World Heritage sites in the United States infringes on national sovereignty.

Ultimately, however, U.S. participation in the Convention does not give the United Nations authority over U.S. World Heritage sites or related land-management decisions. There are currently 21 World Heritage Sites in the United States, including the Statue of Liberty, Grand Canyon, and Everglades National Park.[52]

Pending U.S. World Heritage Site Nominations. Some Members of Congress are concerned about the possible impact of the U.S. withholding (and subsequent loss of a vote in the GC) on several U.S. World Heritage sites currently being considered for inscription on the World Heritage List (the List). In June 2014, for example, the UNESCO World Heritage Committee is expected to consider Poverty Point State Historic Site and National Monument in West Carroll Parish, Louisiana, for inclusion on the List.[53] At this point, it is unclear whether the U.S. withholding will impact the inscription of U.S. sites. In an effort to address this issue, some Members of Congress introduced legislation that would fund the World Heritage Program. In July 2013, for example, the Senate Committee on Appropriations adopted an amendment, by a vote of 19-11, which stated that funds appropriated for "international contributions for scientific, educational, and cultural activities may be available only to the World Heritage Fund." The amendment was not included in FY2014 foreign operations appropriations legislation (Division J of P.L. 113-76).

Effectiveness of Funding Restrictions

The U.S. financial withholding from UNESCO has raised broader issues about the effectiveness of the legislative restrictions that prohibit U.S. contributions to U.N. entities that admit Palestine as a member. In a March 2012 hearing before a House appropriations subcommittee, for example, then-U.S. Permanent Representative to the United Nations Susan Rice questioned whether the 20- year-old restrictions are still relevant in 2012. Specifically, she stated that the Israeli-Palestinian peace process has changed significantly since the 1990s. Rice emphasized that the original legislation was meant to serve as a deterrent and that, given Palestine's recent admission to UNESCO, it no longer serves this function. She argued that rather than withdrawing from UNESCO, which may jeopardize U.S. interests and priorities, the United States should continue to fund the organization and work from within to persuade other member states to reverse the decision to admit Palestine.[54]

Conversely, some policy makers argue that the U.S. withholding deters Palestinian membership efforts and U.N. member states who might consider voting in favor of Palestine's membership. They argue that if the United States were to modify the legislative restrictions to allow for UNESCO funding, it would undermine U.S. credibility and provide a "green light" for Palestine to apply for membership in entities across the U.N. system. Some might suggest that the General Assembly's November 2012 decision to change Palestine's observer status weakens this argument. Alternatively, some experts argue that the legislation has played a role in preventing Palestine from achieving U.N. membership.

Role of UNESCO in U.S. Foreign Policy

The role of UNESCO, and multilateralism as a whole, in U.S. foreign policy is one of the underlying issues facing policy makers as they consider U.S. funding of and participation in the organization. In addition to concerns regarding Palestinian membership, some critics of UNESCO maintain that its activities do not reflect U.S. foreign policy interests. Specifically, they suggest that the United States should devote its resources to bilateral projects that are more in line with U.S. priorities. They emphasize that the United States regularly contributed nearly one-quarter of the UNESCO budget, yet has only one vote in the General Conference and therefore little influence over how U.S. funds are spent. Some critics are also frustrated by UNESCO's history of perceived anti-American leanings and disproportionate focus on Israel. Moreover, as international organizations and development agencies increase their activities in the educational, scientific, and cultural fields, some U.S. policy makers have questioned whether UNESCO is the most effective organization for addressing these issues. They suggest that to stay competitive in the changing multilateral landscape, UNESCO should reevaluate its mission and the scope of its activities to ensure its relevance.

Supporters of UNESCO maintain that the organization plays a key role in global issues that the United States views as strategic priorities, particularly education, science, cultural heritage, and media freedom. They contend that U.S. participation in and funding of UNESCO allows the United States to influence the organization's budget and activities, as well as pursue U.S. foreign policy objectives in key geographic regions such as the Middle East. Moreover, they emphasize that U.S. participation allows the government to share costs and resources with other governments and organizations. Some experts suggest that if the United States does not participate in or fund UNESCO, it leaves the door open for other countries to influence the scope and direction of UNESCO programs. Many of these other donor countries, some argue, may not share the same values or foreign policy priorities of the United States. Proponents further contend that UNESCO's convening power and perceived neutrality (particularly among developing countries) enhances its effectiveness and credibility, allowing it to undertake global challenges the United States could not address on its own, including coordinating global tsunami early warning systems and protecting World Heritage sites.

Challenges to Reform

UNESCO faces multiple challenges as it seeks to implement substantive organizational reform. A key obstacle is governments' differing perspectives on UNESCO's role in the global multilateral framework. Each country has its own foreign policy priorities, political agenda, and perceptions of how the organization should work. Such differences sometimes lead to fundamental disagreements on budgeting, programming, and, as most recently demonstrated, membership. Some experts contend that these disparate perspectives dilute UNESCO's already broad organizational mandate. For example, the GC and Executive Board often approve new themes, activities, and programs for UNESCO headquarters to implement; however, no additional resources are allocated to implement such activities, and many contend that they are not sufficiently prioritized. Moreover, existing programs widely viewed as weak or incoherent are often not eliminated. This occurs not only across UNESCO, but also within individual sectors, in some cases leading to program duplication.

Compounding this dynamic is the sometimes tenuous relationship between developing and developed countries in UNESCO fora. Each country has one vote in the GC and Executive Board, meaning that developing countries, represented primarily by the Group of 77 (G-77),[55] often have the votes to advance their agendas, which some critics argue can be highly politicized. At the same time, developed countries, including the United States, provide the majority of UNESCO funding, yet do not have a proportionate voice in determining the organization's budget or programs. These countries may seek to influence UNESCO activities by allocating extrabudgetary funding for specific programs. They may also turn to other international organizations to address their educational, scientific, or cultural priorities, which some experts argue may undermine UNESCO's authority and effectiveness, drawing much needed resources away from the organization. Many observers have noted that compared to other IOs such as the World Bank, UNESCO no longer has the comparative advantage in the education sector. A recent assessment by the United Kingdom's Department for International Development (DFID), for example, found that "UNESCO's poor leadership in education in the past has meant that leadership is often assumed by others."[56]

Many observers and policy makers, including some in the United States, have argued that the U.S. decision to withhold funding from UNESCO may spur the organization to implement further substantive reform. Specifically, they contend that the budget shortfall has created an opportunity for member states to improve the organization's overall efficiency and effectiveness by reevaluating UNESCO priorities and streamlining its activities. Some critics, however, suggest that the U.S. withholding has had minimal impact on reform efforts. In their view, UNESCO's primary response to the withholding has been to create new funding streams through various emergency funds rather than implement substantive change.

LOOKING AHEAD

The current and future role of UNESCO as an instrument of U.S. foreign policy remains unclear, and any number of events may influence U.S. actions toward the organization. Prospects for U.S. funding of UNESCO might be viewed in the broader context of fiscal austerity debates. Specifically, some policy makers might be less likely to pursue or advocate U.S. funding of or participation in UNESCO in the current economic climate. The level and extent of UNESCO's response to the U.S. withholding may also influence U.S. policy toward the organization. If UNESCO were to implement substantive reform, streamline its budget and programs, or rescind Palestine's membership, lawmakers might be more likely to consider restoring U.S. funding for the organization.

One of the foremost issues policy makers may face is how, if at all, the United States will engage with the organization given the ongoing financial withholding and loss of a vote in the General Conference. The United States remains a member of the Executive Board; however, its term will expire in 2015. Many policy makers worry that the United States will lose its influence in the organization while continuing to accumulate arrearages. Some observers have suggested that the United States withdraw from the organization as it did in 1984, while others—including the Obama Administration—maintain that the United States should remain engaged with the organization to the extent that it can.

End Notes

[1] This report refers to "Palestine" in the context of the U.N. system. U.N. General Assembly resolution 43/177, adopted December 15, 1988, states, "the designation 'Palestine' should be used in place of the designation 'Palestine Liberation Organization' in the United Nations system ... "

[2] In November 2012, the U.N. General Assembly decided to grant Palestine non-member state observer status by a vote of 138 in favor, 9 against (including the United States), and 41 abstaining. For more information, see the "Effectiveness and Reform" section.

[3] The U.N. system consists of the entities or bodies established by the U.N. Charter, including the United Nations and its principal organs, subsidiary bodies, committees, and commissions; the separate international intergovernmental organizations considered specialized agencies by virtue of completing relationship agreements as provided for in Article 57 of the Charter; and a number of programs and funds established by the U.N. General Assembly under its authority derived from Article 22 of the Charter. For a complete list of the components of the U.N. System, see chart at http://www.un.org/en/aboutun/structure/org_chart.shtml.

[4] For more information on UNESCO activities and programs, see http://www.unesco.org/new/en /unesco/themes/.

[5] Examples of UNESCO institutes and centers include the Institute for Statistics and the International Bureau for Education. For a full list, see http://www.unesco.org /new/en/unesco/about-us/where-we-are/institutes-and-centres/.

[6] The GC, for example, has a General Committee that steers the work of each GC session, as well as four other committees that address issues ranging from participant credentials to legal issues. The Executive Board's three committees include the Special Committee, which evaluates UNESCO activities; the Committee on Conventions and Recommendations, which considers the periodic reports of members on the implementation of UNESCO recommendations and conventions; and the Committee on NGOs, which promotes the input of NGOs on UNESCO's work. For more information on the CR Committee, see the "Effectiveness of Funding Restrictions" section.

[7] For example, the UNESCO/NGO Collective Consultation on Higher Education, composed of about 60 NGOs representing all areas of the higher education community, acts as a think tank to assist UNESCO in the orientation and implementation of its higher education programs. In the private sector, UNESCO has worked with L'Oreal to improve the role of women in science, and Hewlett-Packard to alleviate "brain drain" in southeast Europe. It also works with IGOs such as the EU to address the teacher gaps in African countries, and the Inter-American Development Bank to develop World Heritage sites in Peru.

[8] U.N. system-wide mechanisms promoting coordination include (1) the Chief Executives Board, a high-level coordination mechanism, chaired by the Secretary-General, designed to bring together 29 heads of U.N. entities to approve policy statements on behalf of the United Nations, and (2) the U.N. Development Group, composed of the 32 U.N. entities that address development.

[9] The establishment of National Commissions is authorized under Article VII of the UNESCO constitution. For more information on the U.S. Commission, see the "U.S. Policy" section.

[10] See the "Effectiveness and Reform" section for more information on Palestinian membership.

[11] For more information on these laws, see the "U.S. Policy" section.

[12] For the first time, as a result of contributions to the Multi-Donor Fund, UNESCO received more voluntary contributions ($391 million) than assessed contributions to the regular budget ($352.9 million) in 2012. See *UNESCO Annual Report, 2012*, UNESCO, 2013, pp. 110-112.

[13] Drawn from (1) "Facts and Figures: UNESCO's Response to the Financial Crisis," UNESCO website, 2013; (2) "Financial Report & Audited Consolidated Financial Statements – 2012," UNESCO, 2013; and (3) UNESCO document, 190 EX/34, *Financial Situation of the Organization and its Implications for the Implementation of the 36 C/5, Report by the Director-General on the Cashflow Situation of the Organization,* September 7, 2012.

[14] "Address by Ms. Irina Bokova on the occasion of the opening of the 192nd session of the Executive Board," UNESCO, September 30, 2013 (UNESCO document, DG/2013/142 Rev.).

[15] Steve Erlanger, "Cutoff of U.S. Money Leads UNESCO to Slash Programs and Seek Emergency Aid," *New York Times*, October 11, 2012.

[16] This change in observer status is a largely symbolic act. Although Palestine has the term "state" in its current designation, it is not a member of the United Nations. As such, it does not have the right to vote or call for a vote in the General Assembly. Palestine has maintained many of the capacities it had as an observer entity—including participation in Assembly debates and the ability to co-sponsor draft resolutions and decisions related to proceedings on Palestinian and Middle East issues. For more information, see CRS Report RL34074, *The Palestinians: Background and U.S. Relations*, by Jim Zanotti.

[17] U.S. Mission to UNESCO Press Release, "Statement on Syria and the CRR," January 2012.

[18] UNESCO document, 190 EX/22, *Report of the Joint Inspection Unit on the Management and Administration of UNESCO,* August 13, 2012.

[19] Nicholas Burnett, "UNESCO Education: Political or Technical? Reflections on Recent Personal Experience," *International Journal of Educational Development,* Vol. 31, 2011, pp. 315-318.

[20] Aaron Benavot, "Imagining a Transformed UNESCO with Learning at its Core," *International Journal of Educational Development*, Vol. 31, 2011, pp. 558-561.

[21] This does not include extrabudgetary funding, which often supports a range of education programs earmarked by donors.

[22] UNESCO document, 36 C/5, *Approved Programme and Budget 2012-2013.*

[23] See UNESCO documents, 182 EX/Decision 24 and 35 C/Resolution 102. The evaluation was undertaken by a cross-regional 11-person team between January and July 2010.

[24] The evaluators further note that examples of successful collaboration are often the result of "informal efforts by committed individuals over institutional barriers to cooperation." UNESCO document, 185 EX/18, *Report on the Independent External Evaluation of UNESCO, Summary*," August 30, 2010.

[25] Ibid.

[26] For more information on broader U.N. reform efforts, see CRS Report RL33848, *United Nations Reform: Background and Issues for Congress*, by Luisa Blanchfield.

[27] In that period, UNESCO adopted a policy of "zero-budget growth," reduced staff levels, decentralized some staff and program operations to the field, increased its focus on education programs, and established an Internal Oversight Service (IOS), which conducts internal

audits, evaluations, and investigations. For more information on reforms, see GAO report 03-565R, *Status of Reforms and Budgets of the United Nations Educational, Scientific, and Cultural Organization,* March 28, 2003; and Karen Mundy, "Educational Multilateralism in a Changing World Order: UNESCO and the Limits of the Possible," *International Journal of Educational Development,* Vol. 19, 1999, pp. 27-52.

[28] For a list of reforms undertaken prior to the publication of the IEE report, see UNESCO document, 186 EX/17, Part II, *Report by the Director General on the Follow-up With Respect to Operational Aspects of the IEE Report*, April 18, 2011, pp. 2-3. For information on UNESCO reform efforts, particularly related to transparency and accountability, see the UNESCO response to the U.S. Mission to the United Nations U.N. Transparency and Accountability Initiative (UNTAI II), February 2013, available at http://www.unesco.org/new/fileadmin/MULTIMEDIA/ HQ/BPI/EPA/images/media_services/Director-General/UNTAI-II_Consolidated-response_Feb2013.pdf.

[29] See UNESCO documents, 187 EX/Decision 17, and 36/C Resolution 104.

[30] "Address by Ms. Irina Bokova on the occasion of the opening of the 192nd session of the Executive Board," UNESCO, September 30, 2013.

[31] A full list of the 87 action points is available in UNESCO document, 187 EX/17 Part I, *Follow-up to the IEE of UNESCO, Report by the Director-General on Progress in Implementation and Monitoring by the Executive Board System,* September 2, 2011.

[32] For more information on the strategy, see UNESCO document, 186 EX/25, April 18, 2011, *Report by the Director-General on the Human Resources Management Strategy.*

[33] For a discussion of challenges facing UNESCO reform efforts, see the "Issues for Congress" section.

[34] U.S. participation in UNESCO is established under P.L. 79-565, which authorized annual appropriations to the organization, and directed the President to set up a U.S. National Commission for UNESCO. Between 1946 and 1984, the United States contributed nearly $458 million to UNESCO in assessed contributions.

[35] Statement by President George W. Bush, 57th U.N. General Assembly, September 12, 2002.

[36] The Mission supports seven direct-hire positions (composed of foreign and civil service), as well as five local staff members. Agencies involved in UNESCO activities include the National Park Service, the National Oceanic and Atmospheric Administration (NOAA), and the Army Corps of Engineers.

[37] Examples of specific projects include those addressing Holocaust education; promoting literacy and education programs for women and girls; researching seismic activities and earthquake engineering; supporting trade and vocational schools in Afghanistan; preserving traditional music of the world; and promoting open access to global maps, among others. These projects were funded primarily through voluntary contributions to UNESCO.

[38] The commission is composed of 50 NGO representatives, seven federal government officials, nine state and local officials, and 15 at-large individuals. More information is available at http://www.state.gov/p/io/unesco/index.htm.

[39] The provisions are codified as notes to 22 U.S.C. 287e.

[40] U.S. Statement in Explanation of Vote on Draft Resolution 9.1 Regarding Membership for Palestine in UNESCO, delivered by U.S. Permanent Representative to UNESCO, Ambassador David T. Killion, October 31, 2011.

[41] "Office of Inspections, Inspection of the U.S. Mission to the United Nations Educational, Scientific, and Cultural Organization, Paris, France," Department of State Office of the Inspector General, Report ISP-I-12-26, May 2012.

[42] Israel also lost its vote in the GC in November 2013 under Article IV of the UNESCO constitution.

[43] See (1) U.S. National Statement by Ambassador David Killion, 37th General Conference, Paris, France, November 8, 2013, and (2) Press Statement by Jen Psaki, U.S. Department of State, "Loss of Vote at UNESCO," November 8, 2013.

[44] The United States is a member of various UNESCO governing mechanisms, including the Executive Board; the Intergovernmental Oceanographic Commission (IOC) Executive Council, and the International Hydrological Program (IHP) Intergovernmental Council.

[45] Although the United States was not a member of UNESCO between 1984 and 2003, it continued to provide voluntary funding to the organization through the IO&P account.

[46] For FY2012, the President requested $78.245 in assessed contributions and $980,000 in voluntary contributions. In FY2013 and FY2014, he requested $78.968 and $77.764, respectively, in assessed contributions. U.S. funding to UNESCO funding was not provided in FY2012 because the United States' calendar year assessment is typically paid by funds from the following fiscal year (e.g., the CY2012 assessment is covered by FY2013 U.S. funding). The United States' CY2012 assessment, which would have been covered by FY2013 contributions, was estimated at about $79 million.

[47] The Administration's proposed legislative language for the waiver in FY2014 is on p. 29 of the Congressional Budget Justification, Vol. 2., Foreign Operations, FY2014, Department of State: *"(p) SPECIALIZED AGENCY WAIVERS.—The President may waive section 414 of P.L. 101-246 and section 410 of P.L. 103-236 on a case-by-case basis, if the President determines and certifies in writing to the Speaker of the House of Representatives, the President Pro Tempore of the Senate, and the Committees on Appropriations that to do so is important to the national interests of the United States."* If Congress had enacted such a waiver, the Administration requested an additional $38.883 million for "FY2012, FY2013, and FY2014 contingent requirements" funding that would cover U.S. arrears accrued in FY2012 and FY2013.

[48] Most recently, the explanatory statement to the Consolidated Appropriations Act, FY2014 (P.L. 113-76; January 17, 2014) states that the bill "does not include funds for an assessed contribution to ...[UNESCO]... which is prohibited due to the application of P.L. 101-246 and P.L. 103-236." (See Congressional Record, Vol. 160, p. H1162, January 15, 2014.)

[49] The Heritage Foundation Issue Brief #3760, "The United States Should Withdraw from UNESCO," by Brett Schaefer, October 19, 2012.

[50] John Irish, "UNESCO Chief Says Funding Cuts 'Crippling' the Organization," *Reuters*, October 12, 2012, and Steven Erlanger, "Cutoff of U.S. Money Leads UNESCO to Slash Programs and Seek Emergency Aid," *New York Times,* October 11, 2012.

[51] For a discussion of steps UNESCO has taken to reduce costs in light of the U.S. financial withholding, see the "Funding and Budget" section.

[52] For a full list of U.S. World Heritage sites, see http://whc.unesco.org/en/statesparties/US/.

[53] In the summer of 2015, the Committee will likely consider the inscription of the San Antonio Missions in Texas, which includes most of San Antonio Missions National Historical Park, as well as the Alamo.

[54] Drawn from "Testimony of Ambassador Susan E. Rice, U.S. Permanent Representative to the United Nations," House Subcommittee on Appropriations for State, Foreign Operations, and Related Programs, March 20, 2012.

[55] The G-77 is a group of 133 member countries that aim to articulate and promote their collective economic interests and enhance their joint negotiating capacity in international fora such as the United Nations.

[56] Multilateral Aid Review: Assessment of the United Nations Educational, Scientific, and Cultural Organization (UNESCO), DFID, November 2011, at http://www.dfid.gov.uk /Documents/publications1/mar/unesco.pdf. UNESCO's response to the review, dated April 2, 2013, is available at http://www.unesco.org/new /fileadmin/MULTIMEDIA/ HQ/BPI/EPA/images/media_services/Director-General/DFID-MAR-EN.pdf.

In: Membership in the United Nations ... ISBN: 978-1-63321-971-7
Editor: Elizabeth Saunders

Chapter 3

INTERNATIONAL MONETARY FUND: BACKGROUND AND ISSUES FOR CONGRESS*

Martin A. Weiss

SUMMARY

The International Monetary Fund (IMF), conceived at the Bretton Woods conference in July 1944, is the multilateral organization focused on the international monetary system. Created in 1946 with 46 members, it has grown to include 188 countries. The IMF has six purposes that are outlined in Article I of the IMF Articles of Agreement: promoting international monetary cooperation; expanding the balanced growth of international trade; facilitating exchange rate stability; eliminating restrictions on the international flow of capital; ensuring confidence by making the general resources of the Fund temporarily available to members; and adjusting balance-of-payments imbalances in an orderly manner.

Congressional interest in IMF activities has increased since the onset of the financial crisis in 2008. IMF lending has surged in recent years, particularly in light of large recent loans to Greece, Ireland, and Portugal. In 2009, major economies agreed to substantially increase the IMF's resources and to move forward on several major reforms at the institution. These include increasing the voting share of emerging economies; revamping the IMF's lending toolkit to introduce greater flexibility and

* This is an edited, reformatted and augmented version of a Congressional Research Service publication, No. R42019, dated July 17, 2014.

create new facilities for low-income countries; and creating a road map for resolving the fast-growing economic imbalances in the global economy between surplus and deficit countries. In late 2010, IMF members agreed to a doubling of IMF quotas, which would require congressional authorization and appropriations.

The United States was instrumental in creating the IMF and is its largest financial contributor. Since voting shares are based on financial contributions, the large U.S. voting share provides the United States veto power over major decisions at the IMF. Both the IMF and its sister organization, the World Bank, are headquartered in Washington, DC.

At the Bretton Woods conference, the IMF was tasked with coordinating the system of fixed exchange rates to help the international economy recover from two world wars and the instability in the interwar period caused by competitive devaluations and protectionist trade policies. From 1946 until 1973, the IMF managed the "par value adjustable peg" system. The U.S. dollar was fixed to gold at $35 per ounce, and all other member countries' currencies were fixed to the dollar at different rates. This system of fixed rates ended in 1973 when the United States removed itself from the gold standard.

The IMF has evolved significantly as an institution since it was created. Floating exchange rates and more open capital markets in the 1990s created a new role for the IMF—the resolution of frequent and volatile international financial crises. The Asian financial crisis of 1997-1998 and subsequent crises in Russia and Latin America revealed many weaknesses of the world monetary system, which have only become more apparent in the wake of the 2008-2009 global financial crisis and the more recent sovereign debt crises in Europe.

This report evaluates the purpose, membership, financing, and focus of the IMF's activities. It also discusses the role of Congress in shaping U.S. policy at the IMF and concludes by addressing key issues, both legislative and oversight-related, that Congress may wish to consider.

INTRODUCTION

This report provides background information and potential policy issues for Congress concerning the International Monetary Fund (IMF, the Fund), which is the central multilateral organization for international monetary cooperation. The United States is the largest financial contributor to the IMF. Congressional interest in IMF activities has increased since the onset of the financial crisis in 2008. IMF lending has surged in recent years, including large loans to Greece, Ireland, and Portugal. Potential policy issues for Congress include the role of the IMF as a lender of last resort, the adequacy of

IMF resources, and the effectiveness of IMF surveillance of financial and monetary conditions in its member countries and of the world economy.

BACKGROUND

Origins

Prior to World War II, there was no negotiated international regime governing international monetary and trade relations. It was the shared view among the allied powers that many characteristics of the international financial system during the period between the first and second world wars, including competitive devaluations, unstable exchange rates, and protectionist trade policies, worsened the 1930s depression and accelerated the onset of the war. To address these concerns, representatives of the 44 allied nations gathered in Bretton Woods, NH, in July 1944 for the United Nations Monetary and Financial Conference. Their goal was ambitious and largely successful—to create a cooperative and institutional framework for the global economy that would facilitate international trade and balanced global economic stability and growth.

At the Bretton Woods conference, Articles of Agreement for the IMF and the International Bank for Reconstruction and Development (IBRD), later known as the World Bank, were drafted and adopted. They entered into force, formally creating the institutions, on December 27, 1945, following the adoption of implementing or authorizing legislation within member countries.[1] The Articles of Agreement of both institutions constitute an international treaty, imposing obligations on member states, which have changed over time.

In the eyes of its founders, the IMF's purpose and contribution to postwar macroeconomic stability were threefold: (1) facilitate trade by restricting certain foreign exchange controls; (2) create monetary stability by managing a fixed (but flexible) exchange rate system; and (3) provide short-term financing to member countries to correct temporary balance-of-payments problems.

The U.S. Senate agreed to the ratification (by the President) of the Fund and Bank Agreements in July 1945. U.S. participation in both organizations is authorized by the United States Bretton Woods Agreement Act, as amended (Bretton Woods Act).[2]

Unique among the founding members, the United States, in the Bretton Woods Act, requires specific congressional authorization to change the U.S. quota or "shares" in the Fund or for the United States to vote to amend the

Articles of Agreement of the IMF or the World Bank. The U.S. Congress, thus, has veto power over major decisions at both institutions.

The Bretton Woods Monetary System

From 1946 to 1971, the main purpose of the IMF was regulatory, ensuring IMF members' compliance with a par value exchange rate system. This was a two-tiered currency regime using gold and the U.S. dollar. Each IMF member government could choose to define the value of its currency in terms of gold or the U.S. dollar, which the U.S. government agreed to support at a fixed gold value of one ounce of gold being equal to $35. Unlike in the classic gold standard period (1880-1914), monetary policy was not strictly restricted by a country's holdings of gold. Member countries were allowed to intervene in the currency market but were obligated to keep their exchange rates within a 1% band around their declared par value.

When currencies (other than the U.S. dollar) came under pressure from short-term "balance of payments" imbalances that normally arose through international trade and finance exchanges, countries would receive short-term financial support from the IMF. In cases where the currency "peg" was considered fundamentally misaligned, a country could devalue (or revalue) its currency. By providing monetary independence limited by the peg, the Bretton Woods monetary system combined exchange rate stability, the key benefit of the 19th century gold standard, with some of the virtues of floating exchange rates, principally independence to pursue domestic economic policies geared toward full employment.[3]

Balance-of-Payments Basics

The balance of payments is an accounting of a country's international transactions with individuals, businesses, and government agencies in that country and those in the rest of the world. It represents the sum of purely financial transactions (capital account) and those arising from the export and import of goods and services (current account), and other unilateral transfers (such as gifts or remittances).

A country's current account should be equal to the sum of the capital account and any unilateral transfers. If a country spends more abroad on goods and services than it receives, it incurs a current account deficit.

The shortfall, or deficit, can be financed by selling assets or borrowing, which involves a private capital inflow into the deficit country (a capital account surplus). If, however, private sources do not cover the current account deficit, then it must be financed by the government through the sale of foreign exchange (official reserves), which is referred to as a balance-of-payments deficit.

With flexible exchange rates, the deficit (or surplus) is corrected by a market-driven adjustment to the exchange rate—that is, it depreciates or appreciates based on demand. No purchase or sale of official reserves by the government is necessary to operate a floating exchange regime. Under a pegged exchange rate system, however, countries cannot alter exchange rate values and so use their foreign exchange reserves to finance the balance-ofpayments deficit, leaving the currency value intact. When a country does not have adequate foreign exchange reserves to finance its balance-of-payments deficit, it can petition the IMF for financial assistance.

The first major challenge to the postwar international monetary system came in the early 1960s. The postwar expansion in international trade and economic growth required an increase in international liquidity, that is, an increase in central bank holdings of the two major international reserve assets, gold and the U.S. dollar. With the economic recovery of Europe well advanced, the slow growth in gold supplies was hampering the growth of international reserve assets. As early as 1960, global foreign dollar holdings exceeded the value of U.S. gold holdings (at $35 an ounce). The system could continue to function as long as countries were willing to settle their balance of payments in U.S. dollars instead of gold.

The international community's response was to create a new international reserve currency, the Special Drawing Right (SDR). The SDR also serves as the IMF's unit of account. Initially defined as equivalent to 0.888671 grams of fine gold, the value of the SDR was switched to a basket of international currencies following the collapse of the Bretton Woods system of fixed parity exchange rates in 1973. The current basket includes the euro, the Japanese yen, the British pound sterling, and the U.S. dollar.

By 1970, a large and prolonged U.S. balance-of-payments deficit was mirrored by its counterpart, large balance-of-payments surpluses in the other major industrial countries. As a result, much of the 1960s was characterized by substantial currency instability, as liberalized capital flows brought about repeated currency crises in the supposedly "fixed" exchange rate Bretton

Woods system. Amid declining confidence in the U.S. dollar, foreign central banks increasingly became reluctant holders of U.S. dollars and began exchanging their dollar reserves for U.S. gold holdings. After several years of instability, the Bretton Woods system of fixed exchange rates finally collapsed in March 1973 when the United States severed the link between the dollar and gold, allowing the value of its currency to be determined by market forces.

From 1973 to the Present

A major purpose of the IMF as originally conceived at Bretton Woods—to maintain fixed exchange rates—was, thus, at an end. Although the IMF had lost its motivating purpose, it adapted to the end of fixed exchange rates. In 1973, IMF members enacted a comprehensive rewrite of the IMF Articles. IMF members condoned the floating-rate exchange rate system that was already in place; officially ended the international monetary role of gold (although gold remains an international monetary asset); and, nominally, but unsuccessfully, made the SDR the world's "principal reserve asset." Henceforth, member countries were allowed to freely determine their currency's exchange rate, and use private capital flows to finance trade imbalances.

The IMF was also given two new mandates, which became the foundation of its role in the post-Bretton Woods international monetary system. The first was for the IMF to oversee the international monetary system to ensure its effective operation. The second was to oversee the compliance by member states with their new obligations to "collaborate with the Fund and other members to assure orderly exchange arrangements and to promote a stable system of exchange rates." Consequently, the IMF transformed itself from being an international monetary institution focused almost exclusively on issues of foreign exchange convertibility and stability to being a much broader international financial institution, assuming a broader array of responsibilities and engaging on a wide range of issues including financial and capital markets, financial regulation and reform, and sovereign debt resolution.

The IMF also increasingly relied on its lending powers, as floating exchange rates and the growth of international capital flows led to more frequent, and increasingly severe, financial crises. Over the past several decades, the IMF has been involved in the oil crisis of the 1970s; the Latin American debt crisis of the 1980s; the transition to market-oriented economies following the collapse of communism; currency crises in East Asia, South

America, and Russia; and, most recently, the global response to the 2008-2009 global financial crisis and the 2010-2011 European sovereign debt crisis.

INSTITUTIONAL ASPECTS

Organizational Structure

The IMF Articles provide for a three-tiered governance structure with a Board of Governors, an Executive Board, and a Managing Director (**Figure 1**).

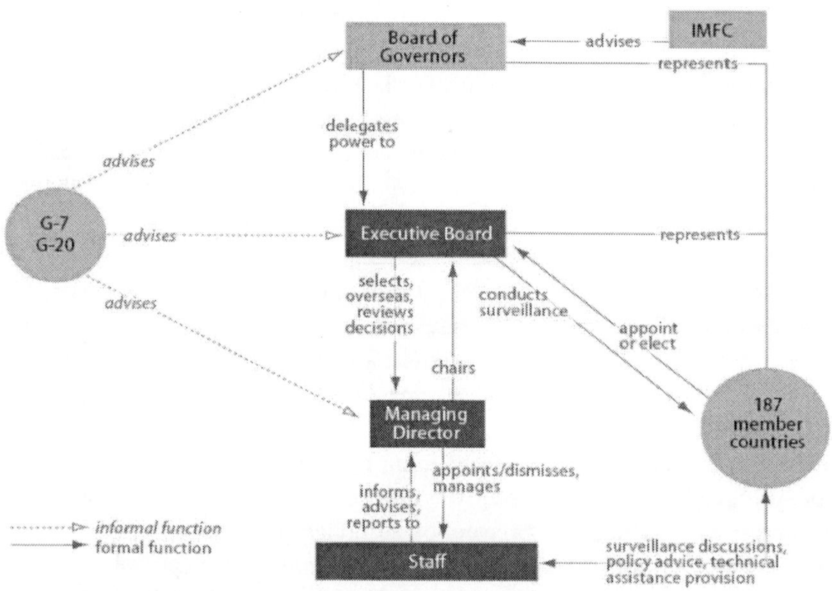

Source: International Monetary Fund, adapted by CRS.

Figure 1. IMF Governance.

The Board of Governors is the highest policy-making authority of the IMF. All countries are represented on the Board of Governors, usually at the finance minister or central bank governor level. IMF Governors usually meet annually at the fall IMF meetings. A committee of the Governors, the International Monetary and Financial Committee (IMFC), meets twice annually to consider major policy issues affecting the international monetary system and makes recommendations to the full Board of Governors. The

Development Committee, a joint committee of the Boards of Governors of the IMF and World Bank, also meets at the same time to consider development policy issues and other matters affecting developing countries. The two committees generally issue communiqués at the close of their meetings, summarizing their findings and recommendations. These often serve as policy guidance to the IMF and the World Bank and as a means for airing views and for coordinating or harmonizing country policies on issues of international concern.

Day-to-day authority over operational policy, lending, and other matters is vested in the Board of Executive Directors, a 24-member body that meets three or more times a week to oversee and supervise the activities of the IMF. The five largest shareholders are entitled to appoint their own Executive Director.[4] The remaining members are elected by groups of countries, generally on the basis of geographical or historical affinity. A few countries— Saudi Arabia, China, and Russia— have enough votes to elect their own Executive Directors. In reforms approved by the Governors in December 2010, the IMF Articles of Agreement will eventually be amended so that the Executive Board will consist solely of elected Directors, doing away with the practice of some member countries appointing their representatives.

The IMF Executive Board selects the Managing Director of the IMF, who serves as its chairman and chief executive officer. The Managing Director is elected for a five-year renewable term of office. The Executive Board also approves the selection of the Managing Director's principal assistants, the First Deputy Managing Director and three Deputy Managing Directors. The Managing Director manages the ongoing operations of the Fund (under the policy direction of the Executive Board); supervises some 2,800 staff members; and oversees the preparation of policy papers, loan proposals, and other documents that go before the Executive Board for its approval.

By tradition, the European countries nominate the IMF Managing Director.[5] The United States has a similar prerogative at the World Bank. The First Deputy Managing Director of the IMF is typically a U.S. citizen. Leadership selection has been a long-standing issue of concern. Emerging economic powers argue that any agreement that grants the leadership position based on nationality limits the pool of potential candidates. During the most recent transition from Dominique Strauss-Kahn to Christine Lagarde, however, non-European countries were unable to coalesce on a candidate, securing the position for a European.

Some analysts argue that calls for a non-European director from the emerging economies mask divides that make it difficult for emerging economies to unite behind one credible candidate. These calls, the argument goes, are part of the larger issue of the influence of emerging economies in the international financial institutions, and could ultimately lead to additional shifts toward emerging economies, despite Europe's hold on the top position. Evidence suggests that some shifts are underway. In July 2011, new Managing Director Lagarde elevated Zhu Min, a Chinese national serving as an advisor to the Managing Director, to Deputy Managing Director.

In addition to the official representation of the Board of Governors and the Executive Board, several other cross-cutting groups of countries are actively involved with the IMF. These include forums such as the Group of Seven (G-7) meeting of the finance ministers,[6] the Group of 20 major economies (G-20),[7] which in 2009 was declared by its members as the premier forum for international economic cooperation,[8] and the Intergovernmental Group of Twenty-Four on International Monetary Affairs and Development (G-24),[9] which coordinates the position of developing countries on monetary and development issues.

Quotas

Quotas are the primary national contribution to the IMF and are the foundation of country representation at the IMF. When a country joins the Fund, it is assigned a quota based on its relative weight in the global economy. Economic considerations include a member's GDP, openness to trade, volume of current account transactions, and level of official reserves.

A country's quota determines:

- **Subscriptions:** the amount of financial resources each member is required to contribute to the Fund;
- **Access to Financing:** the amount of financing a member may receive from the Fund; and
- **Voting Power:** the ability to formally influence the IMF's decisions.

The total of all member countries' quota subscriptions is 238 billion IMF Special Drawing Rights (SDRs), approximately $368 billion.[10] Upon joining the Fund, a country normally pays up to one-quarter of its quota, the so-called "reserve tranche," in the form of reserve assets, widely accepted foreign currencies (such as the U.S. dollar, euro, yen, pound sterling), or special drawing rights (SDRs). The remaining three-quarters are paid in the country's own currency.

Supplemental Facilities

In addition to its regular quota resources, the IMF maintains two standing multilateral borrowing arrangements—the New Arrangements to Borrow (NAB) and the General Arrangements to Borrow (GAB). These are backstop resources intended to temporarily supplement available quota resources and borrowing. If activated, participating creditor countries make loans to the IMF, and the IMF uses those funds to provide loans to eligible countries.

The NAB is a set of credit arrangements between the IMF and a group of member countries and institutions, including advanced economies and a number of emerging market countries. The NAB is the facility of first and principal recourse in circumstances in which the IMF needs to supplement its quota resources. Once activated, it can provide supplementary resources of up to SDR 367.5 billion (about $568 billion) to the IMF. The U.S. commitment to the NAB is $100 billion.[11] The IMF does not hold the NAB funds; rather, the IMF will call on NAB members to provide a percentage of funds that these members have committed if and when the Fund needs to use them. U.S. commitments to NAB are in the possession of the United States until the IMF requests that funds be released. If NAB members choose not to activate the NAB, the GAB, which was established in 1962, allows the IMF to borrow up to $26 billion from 11 industrial countries.

Voting and Influence at the IMF

The Executive Board or Board of Governors of the IMF can approve loans, policy decisions, and many other matters by a simple majority vote. However, a supermajority vote is required to approve major IMF decisions. The supermajority may require a 70% or 85% vote, depending on the issue. A 70% majority is required to resolve financial and operational issues such as the interest rate on IMF loans or the interest rate on SDR holdings. An 85% majority is required for the most important decisions, such as the admission of new members, increases in quotas, allocations of SDRs, and amendments to the IMF's Articles of Agreement.

As **Figure 2** shows, voting at the IMF is highly concentrated, with 10 countries controlling over 50% of the voting shares (**Table 1**). With a voting share of 16.75%, the United States is the only country able to unilaterally veto major IMF decisions (i.e., those requiring an 85% majority). The United States also exercises a substantial amount of informal power at the IMF, given its large quota share and the location of the Fund in Washington, DC.[12] According to one analyst, "the IMF is an instrument of the G-7 countries. There is no example that comes easily to mind of a position taken by the IMF on any systematic issue without the tacit, if not explicit, support of the United States and the other G-7 countries."[13]

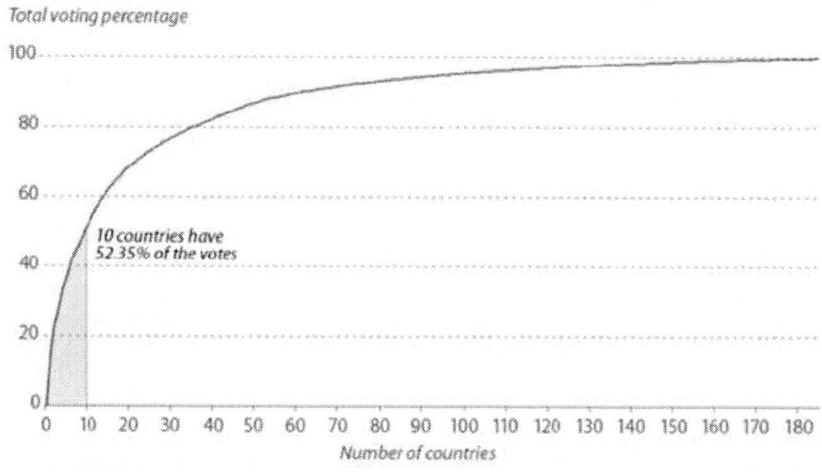

Source: International Monetary Fund.

Figure 2. Concentration of IMF Voting Shares.

The IMF states that its programs are based on purely economic factors, in order to seek an acceptable balance between protecting the interests of individual members and those of the membership as a whole. In practice, however, many analysts contend that the IMF is a highly politicized institution, reflecting the wide power differential between a few advanced economies and the remaining membership. For example, some analysts argue that recent IMF lending to European countries has been greater, and on more lenient terms, than lending provided to developing countries. "History suggests that if this were happening to a poor country or developing country, the rich countries would have voted against [the loan]," argues Arvind

Virmani, the Indian Executive Director at the IMF, commenting about the possibility of fresh IMF support for Greece.[14]

Table 1. IMF Members with Largest Quota and Voting Shares (as of July 10, 2014)

Member	Quota share (percentage)	Voting share (percentage)
United States	17.69	16.75
Japan	6.56	6.23
Germany	6.12	5.81
France	4.51	4.29
United Kingdom	4.51	4.29
China	4.00	3.81
Italy	3.31	3.16
Saudi Arabia	2.93	2.80
Canada	2.67	2.56
Russia	2.50	2.39

Source: International Monetary Fund.

On account of the heavily skewed nature of IMF voting, some analysts also argue that the developing countries with strong political ties to the IMF's largest shareholders get more favorable treatment by the IMF than other developing countries. For example, researchers have found evidence that countries are more likely to receive IMF loans if their voting at the United Nations General Assembly is similar to that of the United States and other advanced economies.[15] At the same time, countries may not seek loans for the IMF, because they are politically unwilling to meet the IMF's economic conditions.

FUNCTIONS OF THE IMF

In practice, the IMF's mandate of promoting international monetary stability translates into three main functions: (1) surveillance of financial and monetary conditions in its member countries and in the world economy; (2) financial assistance to help countries overcome major balance-ofpayments problems; and (3) technical assistance and advisory services to member countries.

Surveillance

The IMF provides surveillance of the international monetary system "in order to ensure its effective operation" and to "oversee the compliance of each member with its obligations" to the Fund.[16] In particular, "the Fund shall exercise firm surveillance over the exchange rate policies of member countries and shall adopt specific principles for the guidance of all members with respect to those policies."[17] The IMF's general surveillance recommendations are not binding or enforceable. The effectiveness of IMF surveillance is dependent on the peer pressure exercised by other IMF member countries, and increasingly the global financial sector, as most IMF analysis of global economic risks is made now public.

The IMF engages in both bilateral and multilateral surveillance. IMF members agree, as a condition of membership, that they will "collaborate with the Fund and other members to assure orderly exchange arrangements and to promote a stable system of exchange rates."[18] In particular, they agree to pursue economic and financial policies that will produce orderly economic growth with reasonable price stability, to avoid erratic disruptions in the international monetary system, not to manipulate their exchange rates in order to attain unfair competitive advantage or shift economic burdens to other countries, and to follow exchange rate policies compatible with these commitments.[19]

Countries are required to provide the IMF with information and to consult with the IMF upon its request. The IMF staff generally meets annually with each member country for "Article IV consultations" regarding the country's current fiscal and monetary policies, the state of its economy, its exchange rate situation, and other relevant concerns. The IMF's reports on its Article IV consultations with each country are presented to the IMF Executive Board, along with the staff's observations and recommendations about possible improvements in the country's economic policies and practices.

In pursuit of its multilateral surveillance function, the IMF publishes numerous reports each year on economic conditions and trends in the world economy. These include three semiannual publications: (1) the *World Economic Outlook*, which provides analysis of the state of the global economy; (2) the *Global Financial Stability Report*, which assesses global financial markets; and (3) the *Fiscal Monitor*, which surveys and analyzes the state of public finances in member countries.

Financial Assistance

Notwithstanding its macroeconomic surveillance, the IMF is perceived as an institution that primarily provides temporary financing to troubled economies. The IMF's financial structure can best be characterized as that of a credit union (see box). IMF member countries deposit hard currency and some of their own currency, from which they can draw the currencies of other countries if they face significant problems in managing their balance of payments. As noted above, supplemental resources are available from the NAB or GAB if quota resources are insufficient.

Mechanics of IMF Financing

The IMF's financing mechanism is rooted in the credit facilities that existed between central banks prior to the IMF's creation. Central banks would borrow from each other with the borrower purchasing the currency of the lender, and paying for it by crediting the lender's account with the borrower in the borrower's currency. Thus, when borrowing from the IMF, a member purchases from the IMF the hard currency of another member in exchange for its own currency. Repayment is effected through a reversal of the original transaction. The member repays the loan by paying the IMF hard currency and repurchasing its own currency that the IMF had acquired. For the IMF to be able to lend, it has available, through members' quota subscriptions and NAB commitments, a pool of hard currency and SDRs. A quarter of a member's quota payment is normally paid in usable assets (SDRs or currencies of other members acceptable to the IMF), and the balance is paid in the member's own currency. When members borrow from the IMF, the pool contains more of debtor members' currencies and less of SDRs or currencies of creditor members. The reverse takes place as members repay their borrowings from the IMF.

Operationally, the IMF decides quarterly, based on the expected pipeline of member borrowings and repayments, which currencies are to be used (and up to what amounts) to finance and repay its lending. The amounts transferred and received by these members are managed to ensure that their creditor positions in the IMF remain broadly even in relation to their quota, which are reported by the IMF on a quarterly basis. The most recent report, covering transactions between August 1, 2010, and October 31, 2010, reported that the U.S. creditor position was 22.5% of total quota available to finance transactions.

The IMF is required by its Articles to ensure that countries' use of its resources will be temporary and that loans will be repaid. Failure of a borrowing country to repay the IMF reduces the availability of financing for all other IMF members. In order to ensure that it gets repaid, the IMF imposes conditionality on its loans. Conditionality is also intended to correct the borrower's current account deficit by bringing about macroeconomic stabilization and economic adjustment.

In the past, there have been debates about whether the austerity conditions that are often the core of IMF conditionality are productive in increasing economic growth. In 2000, one heavily cited paper found that participating in IMF programs lowers growth rates during the program, as would be expected. In addition, however, the study found that once countries leave the program, they grow faster than if they had remained, but not faster than they would have without participating in the IMF program in the first place.[20]

After heavy criticism of the conditions attached to IMF loans to East Asia in the late 1990s, the IMF revamped its conditionality guidelines in 2002. Additional reforms, including new IMF lending instruments based on economic prequalification (ex-ante conditionality) rather than traditional structural adjustment (ex-post conditionality) also address these concerns.[21]

IMF Loan Programs

The IMF has several loan programs. The Stand-By Arrangement (SBA), which provides the bulk of IMF assistance to middle-income countries, addresses short-term balance-of-payments problems and typically lasts one to two years. The Extended Fund Facility (EFF) addresses longer-term balance-of-payments problems requiring fundamental economic reforms and generally runs for three years or longer.

In 2009, following the financial crisis, the IMF created the Flexible Credit Line (FCL). The FCL provides a credit line to countries that have strong economic fundamentals and policies, and that the credit line can be drawn on without new conditionalities being imposed. Unlike the SBA and the EFF, the FCL relies on ex-ante conditionality. As of July 2011, Colombia, Mexico, and Poland have accessed the FCL. In 2010, the IMF introduced the Precautionary Credit Line, now known as the Precautionary and Liquidity Line (PLL), for countries whose financial situations would make them ineligible for the FCL. A country can request a PLL for six months with a limit of five times its quota. The only PLL program approved to date was for Macedonia in January 2011, although many expected some Eurozone countries to request access to credit.

The IMF provides loans to its poorest member countries on concessional repayment terms. These aim to help countries overcome balance-of-payments problems, but their conditionality puts less emphasis on cutting spending and more on economic growth-enhancing reforms. There are three lending facilities for low-income countries:

- The Extended Credit Facility (ECF), which provides flexible medium-term support to low-income members that have protracted balance of payments problems.
- The Standby Credit Facility (SCF), which addresses short-term and precautionary balance of payments needs, similar to the Stand-By Arrangements in regular Fund lending.
- The Rapid Credit Facility (RCF), which provides rapid access at low levels with limited conditionality to meet urgent balance-of-payments needs.

In 2010, the Fund created the Post-Catastrophe Debt Relief (PCDR) Trust Fund to provide debt relief to low-income countries hit by catastrophic natural disasters. The first recipient of the trust was Haiti.

Finally, the Policy Support Instrument (PSI) supports low-income countries that do not want, or need, IMF lending, but seek IMF macroeconomic advice, and a "seal of approval" of their economic policies as a signal to international donors and financial markets. To date, seven countries have received support from the PSI: Cape Verde, Mozambique, Nigeria, Senegal, Uganda, Tanzania, and Rwanda.

Trends in IMF Lending

Prior to the onset of the 2008 economic crisis, many analysts argued that the IMF was on the brink of irrelevance, as booming capital flows and commodity prices allowed the remaining IMF creditors to repay their loans. With developing countries no longer needing IMF lending, and the advanced economies largely ignoring the IMF's surveillance, the Fund's future looked bleak. At the same time, IMF resources, especially when compared to global capital flows, had declined over the past few decades. Prior to the crisis, this raised little concern because demand for IMF resources was low. This view changed quickly in 2008, as the economic crisis worsened, and the IMF's loan portfolio expanded from below SDR 10 billion in 2007 to over to SDR 96.4 billion ($144.6 billion) in February 2013.[22]

Figure 3 illustrates the significant change in the composition of IMF lending since 1970. Advanced economies accounted for over 75% of the IMF credit in 1970, during the waning days of the fixed exchange rate regime. By 1990, their share of IMF credit had dropped to zero, before increasing in the late 1990s (loans to Korea and Russia), and then after the recent financial crisis. In 2010, due to several large European programs, IMF lending to advanced economies accounted for 17% of total lending. Loans to Latin America began rising in the 1970s, but did not increase sharply until the 1980s debt crises, peaking in 1990. Loans increased after 2000 because of three large programs (Argentina, Brazil, and Uruguay), but have since declined, and are now at historically low levels, along with Asian economies.

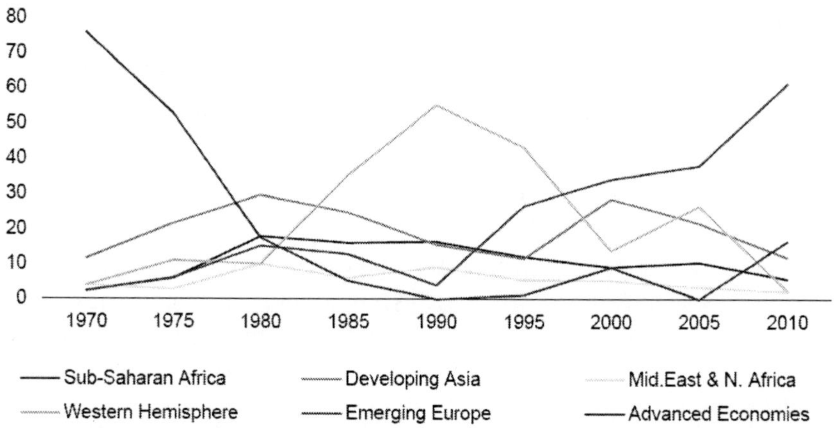

Source: International Monetary Fund.

Figure 3. Outstanding IMF Credit, 1970-2010; (percentage of total outstanding credit).

Another key trend is the increasing size of IMF loans compared to a country's quota. Officially, the amount a country is able to borrow from the IMF is related to the country's quota, its ownership and contribution share in the IMF. In most instances, countries may borrow several multiples of their quota in response to particular circumstances. The conditionality and performance standards attached to a loan become more rigorous and demanding as its size (relative to the borrower's quota) increases. In many cases, deemed exceptional by the IMF executive board at the time, countries have received much larger loans from the IMF than are allowed under normal guidelines. The 2010 loan to Greece, for example, was 3,212% of Greece's quota at the IMF. The 2011 loan to Ireland was 2,322% of its quota.

Technical Assistance

Access to technical assistance is one benefit of IMF membership, accounting for about 20% of the IMF's annual operating budget. The IMF provides technical assistance in its core areas of expertise: macroeconomic policy; tax and revenue policies; expenditure management; exchange rates; financial sector sustainability; and economic statistics. IMF technical assistance supports the development of the productive resources of member countries by helping them to effectively manage their economic policy and financial affairs. The IMF helps these countries to strengthen their capacity in both human and institutional resources, and to design appropriate macroeconomic, financial, and structural policies. About 90% of IMF technical assistance goes to low and lower-middle income countries.[23]

U.S. ENGAGEMENT WITH THE IMF

U.S. Policy-Making Process

As the largest single shareholder of IMF quota (approximately $67.35 billion), and contributor to the NAB ($100 billion), the United States has a leading role in shaping the IMF's lending, surveillance, and advisory operations. While the statutory framework for U.S. participation in the IMF provides the President the authority to appoint the U.S. Governor, Alternate Governor, Executive Director, and Alternate Executive Director, the Department of the Treasury has been delegated responsibility to direct U.S. representatives at the IMF and to take a range of actions with respect to the IMF, including making contributions to capital increases and implementing congressional mandates. Congress is responsible for authorizing and appropriating all U.S. financial commitments to the IMF. The Senate has advise and consent authority over all persons nominated to represent the United States at the IMF.

U.S. participation in the IMF is authorized by the Bretton Woods Agreements Act of 1945.[24] U.S. representatives at the Board of Governors and the Board of Executive Directors are appointed by the President, by and with the advice and consent of the Senate, to terms of five years and two years, respectively. They have the right to remain in office until a successor has been appointed.[25] The Secretary of the Treasury, as a matter of practice, is nominated to serve as the U.S. Governor at the IMF. The Chairman of the

Federal Reserve customarily is nominated to serve as the U.S. Alternate Governor. As discussed above, the Board of Governors has delegated substantial authority to the IMF's Executive Board, which carries out the IMF's day-to-day operations. The U.S. Executive Director and Alternate U.S. Executive Director serve as representatives of the United States to the IMF and present the U.S. government's positions. Executive Directors at the IMF, including those of those of the United States, are employees of the IMF.[26]

When the United States joined the IMF, Congress made an interagency group of executive branch agencies, the National Advisory Council on International Monetary and Financial Problems (NAC), responsible for instructing the U.S. IMF representative, under the general direction of the President. Unless the President overrode their recommendations, policy was determined by a majority vote of agencies involved. The initial interagency procedure did not work well, and in 1965, Congress approved a reorganization act that abolished the NAC as a statutory committee and transferred all of its responsibilities and authority to the President, including the responsibility for instructing U.S. representatives at the IMF. In 1966, President Lyndon Johnson delegated the responsibility to direct U.S. representatives at the IMF to the Treasury Department, where it continues to reside today.[27] The President reconstituted the NAC by executive order, but it became solely a forum where other agencies could advise the Treasury Department about policy concerns regarding U.S. participation in the international financial institutions.[28]

Unlike in a U.S. government department or agency, changes in the IMF's operations cannot be brought about simply by changing U.S. law. As a result, congressional proposals for policy changes in the IMF are formulated as directives to the Secretary of the Treasury to instruct the representative of the U.S. government in the IMF, the U.S. Executive Director, to promote the desired change. These have often been formulated as an instruction to use the "voice and vote" of the United States to achieve the desired goal. Consequently, the term "voice and vote" has become something of a generic or descriptive term for those amendments to U.S. law that seek to bring about specific changes within the IMF. Over the years, "voice and vote" amendments have increased. In the context of the current debate over IMF funding for advanced European economies, questions have arisen over the extent to which congressional policy, as embodied in the "voice and vote" amendments, has been carried out.

Voice and vote amendments can be organized in three broad categories: "policy," "directed vote," and "reporting." Policy mandates seek to foster or advocate certain policies at the IMF by directing the Treasury Department to instruct the U.S. Executive Director to use his or her "voice" and/or "vote" on behalf of the United States at the IMF Executive Board. For example, the U.S. Executive Director is directed to (1) encourage the IMF to adopt internationally recognized worker rights for borrowing countries; (2) encourage and promote the integration of women into the national economies of IMF member countries and into professional positions within the IMF organization; and (3) urge the IMF to encourage member countries to pursue macroeconomic stability while promoting environmental protection.

The second category, directed voting mandates, require that the U.S. Executive Director oppose an IMF loan when a country meets or does not meet certain criteria. In practice, U.S. opposition can take the form of abstaining from voting on, or voting against, the IMF loan under consideration. Examples include when a country has been determined by the President to violate religious freedom, provide support for acts of international terrorism, or engage in the proliferation of nuclear weapons.

Reporting requirements, the third category, require Treasury to report to Congress on various issues related to U.S. participation in the IMF. Congress enacted legislation in 2010, for example, that requires the Treasury Department to report regularly to Congress about economic conditions in heavily indebted advanced economies receiving IMF assistance.[29] These reports are to discuss the debt status of the borrower country, economic conditions affecting its vulnerability and its ability to repay, and its debt management status.

Authorizing and Appropriating U.S. Contributions to the IMF

As discussed above, quota increases are paid to the IMF by transferring 25% of the increase in hard currency and the remainder in national currency, typically through a letter of credit. Both hard currency payments and payments to the IMF under the quota letter of credit result in a budget expenditure only if cash is actually transferred to the IMF. When a transfer is made, however, the United States gets an equal and offsetting receipt—an interest-bearing, liquid international monetary asset, specifically the increase in the U.S. reserve position in the Fund. Under current budgetary conventions, these offsetting transactions are treated as an exchange of assets. As a consequence, they do not result in net budget outlays, and they do not affect the net budgetary position (deficit or surplus) of the federal government. Looked at another way, any debt (liability) incurred through the sale of securities to make this expenditure is balanced by an asset—the U.S. reserve position in the Fund.

Nonetheless, Members of Congress have often provided authorization and appropriations to increase the U.S. quota, reflecting congressional concern about increasing U.S. foreign liabilities, and their impact on the federal budget.

Budgetary treatment for the NAB is identical to that of IMF quota increases: an exchange of assets, having no net effect on the U.S. fiscal position. A drawing by the IMF under the NAB would not constitute a contribution to the IMF's capital and would not, therefore, increase the U.S. reserve position in the IMF. Rather, it would constitute an interest-bearing loan to the IMF. **Table 2** provides U.S. contributions since the IMF's creation, and their budgetary treatment. An **Appendix** provides additional information on the budgetary treatment of U.S. contributions to the IMF.

Table 2. Budgetary Treatment of U.S. Contributions to the IMF

Event	Date Effective	U.S. Contribution (approximate billions of U.S. dollars)	Budgetary Treatment	Appropriation (Yes/No)
Founding Subscription	1945	$2.75	Outlay	No
Quota increase	1959	$1.375	Outlay	No
Establish General Agreements to Borrow (GAB)	1962	$2.00	None	Yes
Quota increase	1966	$1.035	25% outlay, remainder issued as line of credit, outlay on call only	Yes
Quota increase	1970	$1.54	No outlay, exchange of monetary assets	Yes
Quota increase	1978	$2.10	No outlay, exchange of monetary assets	No
Participate in Supplemental Finance Facility	1978	$1.87	No outlay, exchange of monetary assets	No
Quota increase	1980	$5.34	No outlay, exchange of monetary assets	Yes

Table 2. (Continued)

Event	Date Effective	U.S. Contribution (approximate billions of U.S. dollars)	Budgetary Treatment	Appropriation (Yes/No)
Quota increase	1983	$5.58	No outlay, exchange of monetary assets	Yes
GAB increase	1983	$2.45	No outlay, exchange of monetary assets	Yes
Quota increase	1992	$11.92	No outlay, exchange of monetary assets	Yes
Quota increase	1998	$14.55	No outlay, exchange of monetary assets	Yes
Establish New Arrangements to Borrow (NAB)	1998	$3.4	No outlay, exchange of monetary assets	Yes
Ad hoc quota increase	2009	$8.00	Outlay, credit reform scoring adjusted for market risk	Yes
NAB increase	2009	$100.00	Outlay, credit reform scoring adjusted for market risk	Yes

Source: C. Randall Henning, *U.S. Interests and the International Monetary Fund*, Peterson Institute for International Economics, Policy Brief no. 09-12, Washington, DC, June 2009.

POLICY ISSUES FOR CONGRESS

Increased attention to the IMF since the financial crisis has revived long-standing debates about the institution's role in the global economy and the future of U.S. support for the institution. Some analysts argue that with the end of the pegged-exchange rate system, the IMF is no longer needed and it should be abolished.[30] Others say the IMF is still vital, but needs to be restructured and refocused.[31] Still others suggest that new functions should be added to the IMF and its role in the international monetary system should be expanded.[32]

Events since 2008 have shown that substantial risks remain in the global economy. Global imbalances, exchange rate misalignment, volatile capital flows and exchange rate movements, and the accumulation of large stockpiles of foreign exchange reserves have led many analysts to question the functioning of the international monetary system, and by extension, the future of the IMF.

Two issues that Congress may wish to consider are (1) should the IMF act as an international lender of last resort; and (2) are the resources of the IMF adequate to complete this function?

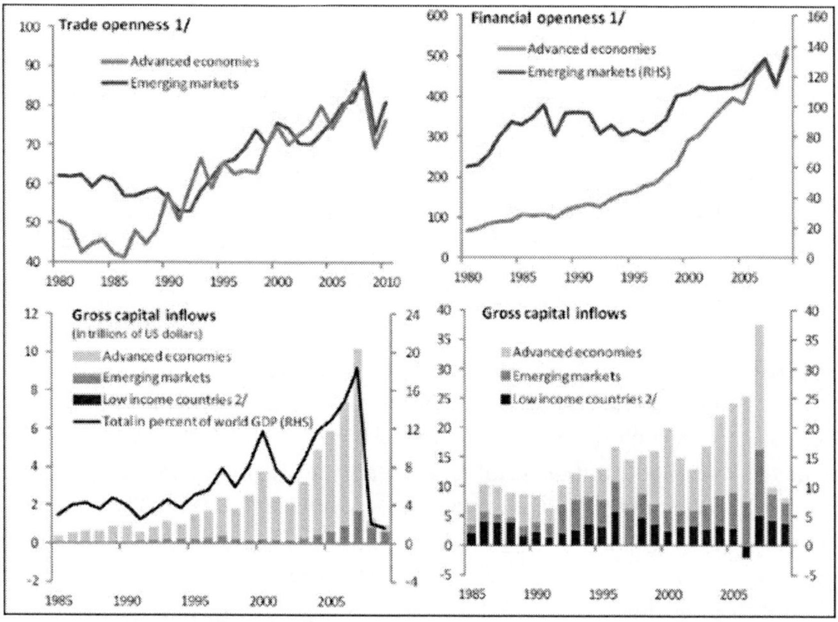

Source: International Monetary Fund.

Notes: (1) Trade openness is the sum of exports and imports as a share of GDP. Financial openness is the sum of external assets and liabilities as a share of GDP. (2) As classified in the IMF *World Economic Outlook.*

Figure 4. Increasing Global Linkages and Risks; (percent of GDP, unless otherwise indicated).

A central challenge for the global economy, according to some analysts, is the lack of an international lender of last resort that has access to sufficient finance to prevent a systemic global financial crisis.[33] Cross-border financial integration has brought many benefits, through trade and increased access to financing, but has also increased the risk of contagion, whereby a crisis may spread beyond its borders to other, seemingly stable economies. This is especially evident among advanced economies, where many analysts argue that the proliferation of credit in the financial system—among advanced economies, gross assets and liabilities are 500% of GDP—reflects significant economic distortions in the underlying economies. As the recent 2008 financial crisis illustrated, a single event, the bankruptcy of Lehman Brothers, can trigger a sharp contraction of global capital flows in such a highly connected global economy (**Figure 4**).

The challenge facing the international monetary system, and thus the IMF, is described by economist Maurice Obstfeld:

> In a world of integrated financial centers and multiple currencies, the boundaries within which a central bank can function as a last-resort lender no longer correspond to the boundaries within which a liquidity shortage *in its currency* can arise. Furthermore, the globally interdependent nature of modern financial relationships ensures that market turmoil *outside* the central bank's jurisdiction may well migrate *inside*. This is the basic problem.[34]

While many emerging and some advanced economies drew on IMF resources during the recent financial crisis, the majority resorted to an ad hoc network of central bank swap arrangements. At the height of the crisis, in the face of a massive global shortage of dollars, the U.S. Federal Reserve deployed over $600 billion in global liquidity to many other advanced and emerging economies, double the available resources of the IMF. The European Central Bank (ECB) set up €250 ($360) billion in swap lines, of which about €200 ($288) billion was with the U.S. Fed. In October 2008, the Fed also authorized swap lines of $30 billion each to four emerging economies with large exposure to U.S. financial institutions, Brazil, South Korea, Mexico, and Singapore. Thus, the Fed, and not the IMF, was the de facto lender of last resort for major economies. At the same time, several other countries, primarily in Asia, relied on their accumulation of foreign exchange reserves built up during the 2000s to prevent their economies from collapsing due to the liquidity crisis.

While central bank swap lines and self-insurance through reserve accumulation were effective in mitigating the effects of the crisis, and restoring liquidity in the global economy, the costs associated with these mechanisms are substantial, both for individual countries and for the system as a whole.[35] By their very nature, the Fed and ECB swap lines were selective, and subject to domestic monetary policy, as well as political pressure. It is uncertain whether the United States will be willing to play this role again in the future. Large accumulation of foreign exchange reserves is expensive, since they typically earn little interest and are susceptible to exchange rate risk. They also contribute to systemic instability, by creating excessive demand for reserve currencies, thus putting downward pressure on interest rates in the economies of reserve currencies, such as the U.S. dollar. Large swings in official portfolios of foreign exchange reserves can also have significant impact on exchange rates and the price of sovereign bonds.

Some analysts have proposed improving the Fund's lender of last resort function. For example, one recent study proposed three main elements of what such reform could look like: (1) an automatic trigger to access the facility; (2) unilateral country prequalification to the facility during Article IV consultations; and (3) liquidity funded by the world's "issuers of last resort."[36]

When considering expanding the role of the IMF, however, the concept of moral hazard has often been considered. As IMF lending increased after the financial crisis, especially after the large loans to Greece, Ireland, and Portugal, many observers, including some Members of Congress, raised concerns that financing by the IMF, particularly emergency financing provided during financial crises, encouraged the very behavior that it sought to prevent. Simply put, IMF lending may send the wrong signals to government officials. According to this view, in the best-case scenario, countries are spared the worst consequences of their poor economic decisions. In other cases, the IMF program may not stabilize the crisis, further indebting the crisis-afflicted country.

Other analysts argue that, as the 1994-1995 Mexican crisis, the 1997-1999 Asian crisis, and the recent 2008 crisis have demonstrated, residents of IMF-recipient countries suffer painful consequences of a forced economic adjustment. The policy question is whether economic pain is mitigated by external financial support tied to a conditional economic adjustment program. A different type of "moral hazard" also arises with regard to investors. Does the existence of an emergency financial mechanism encourage private investors to take on risks that they might otherwise shun in an attempt to reap greater financial returns? In this context, some are troubled that, as a by-product of a "bailout," professional investors, who took on higher risks and were probably rewarded with higher returns, are made whole.

IMF conditionality and pre-qualification of IMF loans might reduce concerns about moral hazard. Edwin Truman at the Peterson Institute for International Economics argues that the IMF's role can be improved, addressing moral hazard at the same time, through a "comprehensive prequalification" process where the Fund presents "policy terms for lending" to every member country potentially eligible to borrow from the IMF, based on the IMF's bilateral and multilateral economic surveillance.[37]

Adequacy of IMF Resources

To address the increased demand for IMF resources, world leaders at the spring 2009 G-20 meeting in London agreed to substantially boost the IMF's lending capacity, primarily by a $500 billion increase in the size of the NAB. The Obama Administration proposed that the United States contribute up to $100 billion.[38] The requisite authorizations and appropriations were included in the FY2009 Spring Supplemental Appropriations for Overseas Contingency Operations (P.L. 111-32).

One of the reasons that world leaders increased IMF resources in 2009 via the NAB, and not through an increase in quotas, was long-standing frustration among emerging market economies that, after years of sustained economic growth, their representation at the IMF did not reflect their current economic position in the world economy.[39] Simply put, many emerging economies were unwilling to increase the IMF's quota resources, unless there was also a shift in their share of IMF quota relative to the advanced economies that had traditionally dominated the institution. At the same time, a broad consensus has emerged that some European countries are over-represented at the IMF compared to their share of global GDP, especially in light of their representation on the Executive Board. European countries have three full seats on the IMF Executive Board, and currently chair or co-chair seven of the group constituencies.

At the April 2010 G-20 meetings, leaders pledged a shift of at least 5% of the IMF quota share to under-represented countries. On November 11-12, 2010, IMF member states agreed on a package of reforms, the core of which is a doubling of overall IMF quota to about $755 billion. In addition, there would be a significant shift of voting power to dynamic emerging market economies. If the reforms are implemented, the 10 largest members of the IMF will consist of the United States; Japan; the four largest European economies (France, Germany, Italy, and the United Kingdom); and Brazil, China, India, and Russia.

The quota increase is expected to come via a repositioning of the NAB resources that were pledged in 2009. As part of the new quota increase to be completed by September 2012, member countries' commitments to the NAB are expected to be proportionally reduced to fund the increase in their quota.

Action by Congress will likely be required for the United States to participate in this plan.[40] According to one analyst, for the United States to participate in the quota increase, Congress would need to authorize a shift of about $65 billion from the funds appropriated for increased U.S. IMF participation in the FY2009 Supplemental Appropriations Act.[41] In addition to increasing the size and composition of IMF quota, there was also agreement on some governance reform of the IMF Executive Board, which would also need congressional approval since the IMF's Articles must be amended for them to take effect. These include

- the transfer of two European chairs to emerging market countries;
- the move to an all-elected Executive Board, eliminating the practice of appointing Executive Directors and allowing all countries to participate in Executive Director elections;[42] and
- establishment of a second alternate Executive Director position for multi-country constituencies with at least seven countries.[43]

The quota and governance reforms are interlinked, and cannot be implemented separately. A double majority of the IMF membership (voting power and number of total members) is required to adopt the reforms. For the quota increase, IMF members representing at least 70% of IMF contributions must consent to the increase. The governance reforms must be agreed by three-fifths of the IMF's 188 members (113 members) having 85% of the IMF's total voting power. In many cases (including the United States) this involves parliamentary approval. Since the United States has voting power of 16.75%, the reforms cannot become effective without ratification by the United States.

APPENDIX. U.S. CONTRIBUTIONS TO THE IMF AND THE FEDERAL BUDGET

When the United States joined the IMF, and for the first two quota increases, U.S. contributions were appropriated and recorded as an outlay on the federal budget. In 1967, the President's Commission on Budget Concepts recommended that U.S. transfers to the IMF be reflected on the federal budget as an exchange of monetary assets of equivalent value to the United States from the IMF, and therefore that they not be recorded in the federal budget as an outlay.

At the time of the next IMF quota increase, which became effective on October 30, 1970, the new budgetary concepts applicable to U.S. transactions with the IMF were not fully implemented. As a result, the transaction was treated as an exchange of assets rather than as an outlay in the official budget, as recommended by the President's Commission on Budget Concepts. For the next quota increase, which became effective in 1978, the U.S. share was subject to the budgetary treatment recommended by the commission: the quota increase was an exchange of monetary assets involving no budgetary outlay and requiring no appropriation.

At the time of congressional debate on the 1980 quota increase, Congress and the Administration agreed to incorporate appropriations legislation to reflect the fact that U.S. commitment to the IMF represented a line of credit. As such, Congress wanted control over the amount of contingent liability the United States undertook through its participation in the IMF. Since the United States received an equal asset at the IMF, and nobody could predict whether there would be any eventual outlays, a compromise was reached whereby U.S. contributions to the IMF (either quota or NAB) would score as budget authority (an act of appropriations would be required), but the contributions would continue to be scored as zero (i.e., no cost) on the federal budget, thus incurring no budget outlays (no effect on deficits/surplus).

In spring 2009, President Obama requested an increase in U.S. contributions to the IMF. When the request was transmitted to Congress, President Obama argued that treatment for U.S. contributions to the IMF should revert to the pre-1980 standard, and thus neither require budget authority nor incur any outlays. While many agreed with the Administration that it was unusual to record budget authority and not outlays, some Members of Congress raised concerns about not scoring any outlays for additional U.S. contributions to the IMF. They argued that such a method did not correctly reflect the degree of risk of the IMF defaulting on the U.S. contribution, given the current economic turmoil.

After several months of negotiation, on May 12, 2009, the White House and Congress reached an agreement to treat the U.S. subscription to the IMF as a line of credit for budgetary purposes. The Federal Credit Reform Act of 1990 provides that when the U.S. government makes a loan, it does not need to include the full face value of the loan in the federal budget. Rather, Congress must appropriate the estimated subsidy cost, an amount equal to the amount the U.S. government might lose from these loans as a consequence of defaults.[44] This procedure is used throughout the federal budgeting process. Unlike IMF quota increases since 1967, the U.S. contribution would be scored as a loan for budgetary purposes under the existing credit reform legislation with a commensurate budgetary impact. In the law authorizing U.S. participation in the new IMF funding plans, the FY2009 Spring Supplemental

Appropriations for Overseas Contingency Operations, Congress subsequently appropriated $5 billion as a loan loss reserve to cover the risk associated with the new U.S. payments to the IMF.[45]

End Notes

[1] The third pillar of the postwar economic agenda, negotiation on multilateral rules to liberalize and govern international trade, was not completed until the 1947 General Agreement on Tariffs and Trade (GATT). In 1995, the GATT was succeeded by the World Trade Organization (WTO).

[2] P.L. 79-171, 22 U.S.C. 286 et. seq.

[3] Ibid.

[4] The five largest shareholders of the IMF are the United States, Japan, Germany, France, and the United Kingdom.

[5] For more information, see CRS Report R41828, *International Monetary Fund: Selecting a Managing Director*, by Martin A. Weiss.

[6] The members of the G-7 are Canada, France, Germany, Italy, Japan, the United Kingdom, and the United States.

[7] The members of the G-20 are Argentina, Australia, Brazil, Canada, China, France, Germany, India, Indonesia, Italy, Japan, Mexico, Russia, Saudi Arabia, South Africa, Korea, Turkey, the United Kingdom, the United States, and the European Union, which is represented at the leaders' level by the presidents of the European Union and the European Commission and at the finance level by the rotating presidency of the European Council and the European Central Bank.

[8] CRS Report R40977, *The G-20 and International Economic Cooperation: Background and Implications for Congress*, by Rebecca M. Nelson.

[9] The members of the G-24 are Algeria, Argentina, Brazil, Colombia, Côte d'Ivoire, the Democratic Republic of Congo, Egypt, Ethiopia, Gabon, Ghana, Guatemala, India, Iran, Lebanon, Mexico, Nigeria, Pakistan, Peru, Philippines, South Africa, Sri Lanka, Syria, Trinidad and Tobago, and Venezuela.

[10] International Monetary Fund, "IMF Members' Quotas and Voting Power," and "IMF Board of Governors," available at http://www.imf.org/external/np/sec/memdir/members.aspx.

[11] To meet the U.S. $100 billion commitment to the expanded NAB, as well as an $8 billion increase in the U.S. quota at the IMF, Congress appropriated $5 billion in the FY2009 Spring Supplemental Appropriations for Overseas Contingency Operations (P.L. 111-32).

[12] Randall W. Stone, *Controlling Institutions: International Organizations and the Global Economy* (New York: Cambridge University Press, 2011).

[13] Lex Rieffel, *Restructuring Sovereign Debt: The Case for Ad-Hoc Machinery* (Brookings Institution Press, Washington, DC, 2003).

[14] Alan Beattie, "IMF Warned over fresh Greek Loan," *Financial Times*, July 8, 2011.

[15] Strom Thacker, "The High Politics of IMF Lending," *World Politics*, vol. 52 (1999), pp. 38-75. See also Axel Drehar, Jan-Egbert Sturm, and James Raymond Vreeland, "Global Horse Trading: IMF Loans for Votes in the United Nations Security Council," *European Economic Review*, vol. 53 (2009), pp. 742-757.

[16] Article IV, Section 3.

[17] Ibid.

[18] Article IV, Section 1.

[19] Ibid.

[20] Adam Przeworski and James Vreeland, "The effect of IMF programs on economic growth," *Journal of Development Economics*, vol. 62 (2000).

[21] Olivier Jeanne, *Dealing with Volatile Capital Flows*, Peterson Institute for International Economics, Working Paper PB10-180, Washington, DC, July 2010.

[22] For more information, see CRS Report RS22976, *The Global Financial Crisis: The Role of the International Monetary Fund (IMF)*, by Martin A. Weiss.

[23] International Monetary Fund, *Fact Sheet: IMF Lending*, March 30, 2011.

[24] 22 U.S.C. 286 et seq.

[25] 22 U.S.C. 286a (a), (b).

[26] Federal law limits the salaries that IMF may pay the U.S. representatives, capping them at the rate of level IV of the Executive Schedule for the U.S. Executive Director and level V for the Alternate U.S. Executive Director.

[27] Executive Order 11269 of February 14, 1966, as amended, specifically delegates to the Secretary of the Treasury the President's authority to instruct representatives of the United States to the international financial organizations and to provide the U.S. government's consent with respect to IMF decisions. In addition, 22 U.S.C. 6593 specifically provides the Department of the Treasury with the primary responsibility to continue to coordinate "activities relating to United States participation in international financial institutions and relating to organization of multilateral efforts aimed at currency stabilization, currency convertibility, debt reduction, and comprehensive economic reform programs."

[28] Since 1999, Congress has required that Treasury, as Chairman of the NAC, annually report to Congress on several topics related to U.S. participation in the international financial institutions, including an assessment of the effectiveness of the major policies and operations of the international financial institutions; the major issues affecting United States participation; progress made and steps taken to achieve U.S. policy goals (including major policy goals embodied in current law).

[29] For more information, see CRS Report R41239, *Frequently Asked Questions about IMF Involvement in the Eurozone Debt Crisis*, coordinated by Rebecca M. Nelson, p. 22.

[30] Amar Bhide and Edmund Phelps, "More Harm Than Good: How the IMF's Business Model Sabotages Properly Functioning Capitalism," *Newsweek*, July 11, 2011.

[31] Edwin Truman, *On What Terms is the IMF Worth Funding?*, Peterson Institute for International Economics, WP 08- 11, Washington, DC, December 2008.

[32] Barry Eichengreen, *Out-of-the-Box Thoughts on the International Financial System*, International Monetary Fund, Working Paper no. 09-116, Washington, DC, May 2009.

[33] In a national economy, this function is typically provided by the central bank. See CRS Report RS21986, *Federal Reserve: Lender of Last Resort Functions*, by Marc Labonte.

[34] Maurice Obstfeld, *Expanding Gross Asset Positions in the International Monetary System*, remarks at the Federal Reserve Bank of Kansas City symposium on "Macroeconomic Challenges: The Decade Ahead," Jackson Hole, Wyoming, August 26-28, 2010.

[35] Maurice Obstfeld, Jay C. Shambaugh, and Alan M. Taylor, *Financial Instability, Reserves, and Central Bank Swap Lines in the Panic of 2008*, National Bureau of Economic Research, NBER Working Paper No. 14826, March 2009.

[36] Eduardo Fernandez-Arias and Eduardo Levy Yeyati, *Global Financial Safety Nets: Where Do We Go from Here?*, Inter-American Development Bank, IDB Working Paper 231, November 2010.

[37] Edwin Truman, *The IMF as International Lender of Last Resort*, Peterson Institute for International Economics, Real Time Economic Issues Watch, October 12, 2010.

[38] CRS Report R40578, *The Global Financial Crisis: Increasing IMF Resources and the Role of Congress*, by Jonathan E. Sanford and Martin A. Weiss.

[39] CRS Report RL33626, *International Monetary Fund: Reforming Country Representation*, by Martin A. Weiss.

[40] For more information, see CRS Report R42844, *IMF Reforms: Issues for Congress*, by Rebecca M. Nelson and Martin A. Weiss.

[41] Edwin Truman, IMF Governance Reform: A "Pretty Good" Step in the Right Direction, *Peterson Institute for International Economics*, November 8, 2010.

[42] Currently, members holding the five largest voting positions at the Fund appoint an Executive Director and are unable to participate in the elections that decide nominated Executive Directors.

[43] International Monetary Fund, "Factsheet: IMF Quotas," March 3, 2011.

[44] See out-of-print CRS Report RL30346, *Federal Credit Reform: Implementation of the Changed Budgetary Treatment of Direct Loans and Loan Guarantees*, by James M. Bickley (available upon request).

[45] CRS Report R40531, *FY2009 Spring Supplemental Appropriations for Overseas Contingency Operations*, coordinated by Stephen Daggett and Susan B. Epstein.

In: Membership in the United Nations ... ISBN: 978-1-63321-971-7
Editor: Elizabeth Saunders

Chapter 4

UNITED NATIONS REFORM: BACKGROUND AND ISSUES FOR CONGRESS*

Luisa Blanchfield

SUMMARY

Since its establishment in 1945, the United Nations (U.N.) has undergone numerous reforms as international stakeholders seek ways to improve the efficiency and effectiveness of the U.N. system. During the past two decades, controversies such as corruption in the Iraq Oil-For-Food Program, allegations of sexual abuse by U.N. peacekeepers, and instances of waste, fraud, and abuse by U.N. staff have focused attention on the need for change and improvement of the United Nations. Many in the international community, including the United States, continue to promote substantive reforms. The second session of the 113th Congress may focus on U.N. reform as it considers appropriate levels of U.S. funding to the United Nations and monitors the progress and implementation of ongoing and previously approved reform measures.

Generally, Congress has maintained a significant interest in the overall effectiveness of the United Nations. Some Members are particularly interested in U.N. Secretariat and management reform, with a focus on improving transparency and strengthening accountability and internal oversight. In the past, Congress has enacted legislation that links U.S. funding of the United Nations to specific U.N. reform benchmarks.

* This is an edited, reformatted and augmented version of a Congressional Research Service publication, No. RL33848, dated January 13, 2014.

Supporters of this strategy contend that the United Nations has been slow to implement reforms and that linking payment of U.S. assessments to progress on U.N. reform is the most effective way to motivate member states to efficiently pursue comprehensive reform. Opponents argue that tying U.S. funding to U.N. reform may negatively impact diplomatic relations and could hinder the United States' ability to conduct foreign policy.

In September 2005, heads of U.N. member states met for the World Summit at U.N. Headquarters in New York to discuss strengthening the United Nations through institutional reform. The resulting Summit Outcome Document laid the groundwork for a series of reforms that included enhancing U.N. management structures; strengthening the U.N. Security Council; improving U.N. system coordination and coherence; and creating a new Human Rights Council. Since the Summit, U.N. member states have worked toward implementing these reforms with varied results. Some reforms, such as the creation of the Human Rights Council and improving systemwide coherence, are completed or ongoing. Others reforms, such as Security Council enlargement and changes to management structures and processes, have stalled or not been addressed.

One of the key challenges facing reform advocates is finding common ground among the disparate definitions of reform held by various stakeholders. There is no single definition of U.N. reform, and consequently there is often debate over the scope, appropriateness, and effectiveness of past and current reform initiatives. U.N. member states disagree as to whether some proposed reforms are necessary, as well as how to most effectively implement reforms. Developed countries, for example, support delegating more power to the U.N. Secretary-General to implement management reforms, whereas developing countries fear that giving the Secretary-General more authority may undermine the power of the U.N. General Assembly and therefore the influence of individual countries.

Generally, U.N. reform is achieved by amending the U.N. Charter or through various non-Charter reforms. Charter amendment, which requires approval by two-thirds of the General Assembly and ratification "according to the constitutional processes" of two-thirds of U.N. member states (including the five permanent Security Council members), is rarely used and has been practiced on only a few occasions. Non-Charter reforms—which include General Assembly action or initiatives by the U.N. Secretary-General—are more common and comparatively easier to achieve.

INTRODUCTION

United Nations (U.N.) reform is an ongoing policy issue for the United States, and may continue to be an area of focus during the second session of the 113th Congress. As the single largest financial contributor to the U.N. system, the U.S. government has an interest in ensuring the United Nations operates as efficiently and effectively as possible. Congress has the responsibility to appropriate U.S. funds to the United Nations and can impose conditions on payments. On several occasions, it has sought to link U.S. funding of the United Nations to specific reform benchmarks.

Since the establishment of the United Nations in 1945, U.N. member states and past secretaries-general have repeatedly attempted to reform the organization. These reform efforts tend to be cyclical, with member states considering waves of new reform proposals every 5 to 10 years. The reform attempts are often initiated by a member state, groups of member states, and/or the current Secretary-General. They have generally focused on three areas of concern: (1) perceived inefficiencies and lack of accountability in the U.N. Secretariat; (2) duplication and redundancy of U.N. mandates, missions, and/or programs; and (3) evidence of fraud, waste, abuse, and/or mismanagement of U.N. resources.

Proposed reforms often reflect the political, economic, and cultural climate of the time. In the 1950s and 1960s, member states focused on increasing membership on the U.N. Security Council and the U.N. Economic and Social Council (ECOSOC) to account for growing U.N. membership.[1] In the 1970s, as the economic and political gap between developed and developing countries grew more pronounced, the General Assembly examined structural changes that would help the United Nations address "problems of international economic co-operation."[2] Due in part to pressure from the United States, U.N. reform initiatives in the 1980s and early 1990s addressed financial and structural issues, with a particular focus on decision-making processes related to the U.N. regular budget, which funds core U.N. activities.[3] Since the early 2000s, reform efforts have been driven by a combination of U.N. budgetary and financial challenges, controversy over mismanagement of the Iraq Oil-For-Food Program, perceived ineffectiveness of U.N. human rights mechanisms, and allegations of sexual abuse committed by U.N. staff and peacekeepers, among other issues.

This report examines reform priorities from the perspective of several key actors, including Members of Congress, the Obama Administration, selected member states, the U.N. Secretary-General, and a cross-section of groups tasked with addressing U.N. reform. It also discusses congressional actions related to U.N. reform and mechanisms for implementing reform, as well as possible challenges facing U.S. policy makers as they consider existing and future U.N. reform efforts.

SELECTED REFORM EFFORTS: 2005-PRESENT

In 2005, U.N. reform efforts gained momentum as heads of state and government met for a World Summit at U.N. Headquarters in New York.[5] The Summit Outcome Document, which was adopted by consensus, laid the foundation for a series of reforms that included improving U.N. management structures; strengthening the Security Council (see **text box**); enhancing U.N. system coordination and coherence; and creating a new Human Rights Council (see **text box**).[6] U.N. member states have worked toward implementing these reform initiatives with varied results. Some reforms are stalled or have not been addressed, while others are underway or completed. Selected reform activities include the following:

- **Mandate Review**. The Outcome Document negotiated by member states at the World Summit called for a systematic review of all U.N. mandates five years or older.[7] Many experts were concerned that existing mandates might be duplicative, no longer relevant, or require unnecessary reporting requirements. Since 2005, member states have been reviewing mandates, but progress has stalled because some countries fear that mandates important to them will be discarded.

Strengthening the U.N. Security Council

For several decades, many U.N. member states have increasingly focused on the question of Security Council reform. The Council is the primary U.N. organ dealing with peace and security issues. As such, it has often played a lead role in addressing conflict and other forms of insecurity throughout the world. Some member states, finding themselves committed to what they may consider Council-imposed decisions, believe the entire U.N. membership needs to have a clearer understanding of Council actions and greater access to the work of the Council.

Many also believe that the Council membership should be enlarged from 15, a number established in the 1960s, to a number commensurate with the increase in U.N. membership.

Security Council reform and enlargement has been actively discussed within the U.N. General Assembly since 1993, when it established an open-ended working group to address the issue. Over the years, consultations and discussions have continued over various aspects of Council reform, including (1) increases in the number of permanent members; (2) increases in the number of nonpermanent members; (3) the status of new permanent members, including extension of the veto to such members; (4) continuation of the veto; or (5) limits on veto use. The Obama Administration has stated that it is open, in principle, to "modest" expansion of both permanent and non-permanent Council members.[4] It maintains that any proposals should be country-specific and follow a step-by-step approach. It also opposes any changes to the current veto structure. In November 2010, President Obama expressed support for India's inclusion as a permanent Security Council member.

- **Internal Justice Administration**. In 2007, the General Assembly adopted a framework resolution to create a new system of internal justice administration. The previous system was criticized for being "slow, cumbersome, ineffective, and lacking in professionalism."[9] Since the new system became operational in 2009, the Tribunal judges have worked through a backlog of cases.
- **Internal Oversight.** The Summit Outcome Document called for strengthening the U.N. Office of Internal Oversight (OIOS). Experts, however, continue to question OIOS's ability to effectively evaluate U.N. activities in part because it depends on funding from the programs that it audits. Some member states maintain that this lack of operational independence could lead to a real or perceived conflict of interest.
- **System-wide Coherence.** To improve coordination and coherence within the U.N. system, in 2007 member states created the "Delivering As One" initiative in eight pilot countries to harmonize U.N. system-wide activities at the country level; and in 2011 they consolidated three existing U.N. entities addressing women's issues into "UN Women," a specialized agency to address gender equality and women's empowerment.

The long-term impact of these and other recent activities remains to be seen. The overall success of these efforts—and any future reform efforts—depends on how effectively the United Nations and its member countries manage and follow through on the implementation of these reforms and how, if at all, they work to correct possible weaknesses or issues that may arise over time.[10]

The U.N. Human Rights Council

In March 2006, the General Assembly adopted a resolution replacing the Commission on Human Rights with a new Human Rights Council. Many governments, including the United States, viewed the Council's establishment as a key component of U.N. reform. The Council was designed to be an improvement over the Commission, which was criticized by many governments and human rights experts when widely perceived human rights abusers were elected as members. Under the George W. Bush Administration, the United States voted against the General Assembly resolution creating the Council and did not run for a seat. It argued that the Council lacked mechanisms for maintaining credible membership.

Since the Council was established, some policy makers have expressed concern with the Council's effectiveness in addressing human rights. Many contend that the Council has focused disproportionately on Israel while failing to address other pressing human rights situations. In mid-2007, for example, members agreed to make the "human rights situation in Palestine and other occupied Arab territories" a permanent part of the Council's agenda. Israel is the only country singled out in this manner. At the same time, others contend that mechanisms such as the universal periodic review process, which aims to evaluate each member state's fulfillment of its human rights obligations, are a potentially effective means for addressing human rights in various countries. Many supporters are also encouraged by the Council's increased attention to human rights situations in countries such as Syria and Cote d'Ivoire. The Obama Administration has criticized the Council for its focus on Israel, but maintains that it is better for the United States to work from within to improve the Council. The United States was elected as a member in 2009 and 2012.[8]

CONGRESS AND U.N. REFORM

Generally, Congress supports the United Nations and its overall mission. It authorizes and appropriates U.S. funds to the organization each year and often uses U.N. mechanisms to further U.S. foreign policy objectives.[11] Congress can also be critical of the United Nations—especially when some Members believe that it may not be running as effectively as it could be. In such instances, Congress may use a wide range of legislative tools to influence and direct U.S. policy at the United Nations. Placing financial conditions or limits on U.S. funding to the United Nations, described in more detail below, is a common congressional approach to U.N reform. Other tools may include considering "sense of the Congress" resolutions; holding hearings to investigate U.N. programs or oversee Administration policies; and considering U.S. nominations for U.N. posts.

Palestinian Membership in UNESCO and the United Nations

UNESCO has received significant U.S. and international attention for member states' decision to admit "Palestine" as a member in October 2011. The Obama Administration and many Members of Congress opposed this action, maintaining that Palestinian statehood can only be realized through direct negotiation between Israelis and Palestinians rather than through membership in U.N. entities. The United States withheld approximately $80 million in FY2012 and FY2013 funding to UNESCO under two laws enacted in the 1990s that prohibit funding to U.N. entities that admit the PLO as a member (§414 of P.L. 101-246), or grant full membership as a state to any organization or group that does not have the internationally recognized attributes of statehood (§410 of P.L. 103-236). In late 2013, the United States lost its vote in the UNESCO General Conference because it did not pay its dues for two consecutive years. The Obama Administration has asked Congress to waive the legislative restrictions prohibiting funding to UNESCO, and has stated that it does not intend to withdraw from the organization.[12]

Palestinian efforts to achieve UNESCO membership are part of broader efforts by PLO Chairman and Palestinian Authority President Mahmoud Abbas to achieve international recognition for Palestinian statehood.

On November 29, 2012, the U.N. General Assembly voted to change Palestine's observer status from "observer entity" to "non-member observer state" by a vote of 138 in favor, 9 against (including the United States), and 41 abstaining. This change in observer status is a largely symbolic act. Although Palestine has the term "state" in its current designation, it is not a U.N. member. As such, it does not have the right to vote or call for a vote in the General Assembly. Palestine has maintained many of the capacities it had as an observer entity—including participation in Assembly debates and the ability to co-sponsor draft resolutions and decisions related to proceedings on Palestinian and Middle East issues.[13]

U.S. Funding as a Mechanism for U.N. Reform

In the past, Congress has used its authority to limit U.S. funds to the United Nations as a mechanism for influencing U.N. policy.[14] In some cases, Congress withheld a proportionate share of funding for U.N. programs and policies of which it did not approve. It has withheld funds from regular budget programs, including the U.N. Special Unit on Palestinian Rights and the Preparatory Commission for the Law of the Sea. Currently, the only proportionate U.S. withholding from the regular budget is for some activities and programs related to the PLO or entities associated with it.[15] In October 2011, the United States withheld funding from the U.N. Educational, Scientific, and Cultural Organization (UNESCO) due to member states' decision to admit "Palestine" as a member (see **text box**).

The overall impact of withholding a proportionate share of assessed payments depends on the origin of the program's funding. If a program is funded by the U.N. regular budget[16] and the United States withholds a proportionate share of its normal contributions, the cost of the program will most likely be covered by surplus regular budget funds. Some U.N. programs are funded from several budgets that may include the U.N. regular budget, specialized agency budgets, and separate conference and administrative budgets. Because of this, it may be more difficult for U.S. proportionate withholdings to have a significant impact because the program's funding comes from several sources. In such cases, a U.S. withholding would have little or no immediate impact on the program's operation or funding levels. If the United States withholds funds from a program funded primarily by member state contributions, however, the impact of the United States withholding or suspending contributions could be greater.

Enacted and Proposed U.N. Reform Legislation in the 112th and 113th Congresses

Members of the 112th and 113th Congresses have sought to tie U.S. funding to U.N. reform, with a particular interest in improving U.N. transparency and management. Two examples of enacted and proposed legislation follow.

Enacted. Section 7049 of the Department of State, Foreign Operations, and Related Programs Appropriations Act, 2012 (Division I of P.L. 112-74; the Consolidated Appropriations Act, 2012) states that the United States shall withhold 15% of its contributions to any U.N. agency if the Secretary of State determines that the agency is not taking steps to (a) publish regular financial and programmatic audits of the agency on a publicly available website and provide the U.S. government with necessary access to such audits; and (b) implement best practices for protecting whistleblowers from retaliation. The Secretary of State may waive these restrictions if it is determined that doing so is in the best interest of the United States. The conditions in Section 7049 were included in the continuing resolution for FY2013 foreign operations appropriations (P.L. 113-6). The Administration did not withhold FY2012 or FY2013 funding for any U.N. entities under this legislation.

Proposed. In October 2011, the House Foreign Affairs Committee (HFAC) reported out H.R. 2829, the United Nations Transparency, Accountability, and Reform Act of 2011, which (1) supported shifting the funding mechanism for the U.N. regular budget from assessed to voluntary contributions, and (2) tied U.S. contributions the United Nations to specific reform benchmarks. (Similar versions of this act, S. 1313 and H.R. 3155, were introduced in the 113th Congress.) The Obama Administration stated that it had some "constitutional concerns" with the bill, contending that "numerous provisions ... would interfere with the President's conduct of diplomacy by purporting to declare 'policy' of the United States, or by purporting to direct United State diplomats to use their 'voice' or 'vote' to advance certain positions, in international negotiations. The Constitution commits to the President the responsibility for formulating the policy of the United States with respect to international bodies."[17]

In addition to withholding a proportionate share of U.S. funding, Congress may consider enacting legislation decreasing or increasing U.S. assessment levels or linking payment of U.S. arrears to policies it favors. In October 1993, for example, Congress directed that the U.S. payments of peacekeeping assessments be capped at 25% (lower than the assessment level set by the United Nations).[18] Congress has also used this strategy to further its U.N. reform policies. Enacted legislation such as the Helms-Biden Agreement linked U.S. assessment levels and the payment of U.S. arrears to reform benchmarks (see **Appendix A** for more information on legislation). As noted in the previous **text box**, some current Members of Congress have proposed shifting U.S. funding from assessed to voluntary contributions.

Perspectives on Linking U.S. Funding to U.N. Reform

Opponents of linking U.S. funding to progress on U.N. reform are concerned that doing so may weaken U.S. influence at the United Nations, thereby undercutting the United States' ability to conduct diplomacy and make foreign policy decisions.[19] Some argue that withholding U.S. assessed payments to the United Nations infringes on U.S. treaty obligations and alienates other U.N. member states. Opponents also note that withholding U.S. funds could have an impact on diplomatic relations outside of the U.N. system. Additionally, some contend that U.N. reform legislation proposals may be unrealistic because the scope and depth of reforms required by the legislation cannot be adequately achieved in the proposed time frames.[20]

Supporters of linking U.S. funding to specific reforms argue that the United States should use its position as the largest U.N. financial contributor to push for the implementation of policies that lead to comprehensive reform. They note that despite diplomatic and political pressures from many countries, the United Nations has been slow to implement substantive reform. Advocates also argue that some previously implemented reforms have proved to be ineffective. They believe that tying U.S. funding to U.N. reform may motivate countries to find common ground on divisive issues. They also emphasize that past legislation that threatened to cut off U.S. funding of the United Nations (such as the Kassebaum-Solomon amendment) was effective, and led to substantive changes in U.N. operations and programs.

POSSIBLE INSTRUMENTS FOR FURTHERING U.S. REFORM POLICY

Congress's influence over U.S. funding of the United Nations is a powerful tool for furthering U.S. reform policy at the United Nations.

However, there may be other strategies for Congress to consider when advocating its reform agenda. These strategies have been widely used by many past and current Members of Congress and Administrations, and include, but are not limited to:

- **Resolutions**—Members of Congress may propose and/or enact simple or concurrent resolutions expressing an opinion, fact, or principle in one or both chambers of Congress. Some Members have used these resolutions to voice an opinion about U.S. policy in the United Nations/or the United Nations itself.
- **Working with the U.N. Secretary-General**—Some previous and current Members of Congress and Administrations have worked to earn the support of U.N. secretaries-general to help advocate their positions. Developing a relationship with the chief administrative officer of the United Nations can be valuable during some negotiations, when the Secretary-General can act as a bridge among member states that disagree on issues. U.S. citizens have also held key U.N. reform-related posts at the United Nations, which some Members of Congress believe may play a role in furthering U.S. reform policy interests.[21]
- **Collaborating with Other U.N. Member States**—The United States may wish to continue to reach out to other U.N. member states to build consensus and form partnerships on reform policies, either within the framework of the United Nations or bilaterally.[22] Observers have noted that U.S. support for certain U.N. reform initiatives can be a liability because some member states may view U.S. support as self-serving. In these cases, the United States may consider encouraging like-minded countries to advocate its reform agenda.
- **Identifying Key Priorities**—The United States may wish to focus on a small number of reform priorities and pursue them vigorously in both multilateral and bilateral fora. It may also consider compromising with other member states on U.N. reform issues that it has identified as lesser priorities.

Many experts have emphasized that U.N. reform is an ongoing process rather than a singular event. With this in mind, the 113th Congress may wish to continue monitoring the implementation and overall progress of ongoing reform initiatives. It may also consider future reforms proposed by member states and the Administration, as well as by Members of Congress or the Secretary-General.

ADMINISTRATION POLICIES

The United States generally supports the mission and mandate of the United Nations. It played a key role in establishing the United Nations in 1945, and serves as one of five permanent members of the Security Council. Some Administrations have been critical of the United Nations, however, and have advocated sweeping reform of the organization.

Obama Administration

Since President Obama took office, his Administration has focused on "re-engaging" with the United Nations.[23] The Administration elevated the status of the U.S. Permanent Representative to the United Nations to a Cabinet-level position that reports directly to the President.[24] It also paid a significant portion of U.S. arrears, and decided to run for a seat on the U.N. Human Rights Council. Many of the Administration's U.N. reform priorities focus on management issues— particularly those related to budget processes and transparency. In various statements and documents, the Administration has highlighted the following areas of priority:

- **enforcing budget discipline** by taking cost-saving measures such as eliminating vacant U.N. posts, freezing U.N. staff salaries, and exploring alternate budget practices;
- **improving transparency and accountability** by strengthening the effectiveness of U.N. bodies charged with evaluating performance and investigating abuses, including the Ethics Office, the Independent Audit Advisory Committee, the Board of Auditors, and the Office of Internal Oversight Services (OIOS);
- **reforming human resources practices** to create a more mobile and merit-based workforce by further streamlining U.N. staff contracting and conditions of service across the U.N. system; and
- **overhauling day-to-day business practices** such as upgrading information technology, and improving procurement procedures, accounting procedures, and budgeting processes.[25]

The Obama Administration has also implemented initiatives within the State Department aimed at evaluating and improving U.N. system transparency and effectiveness. It has continued to support the U.N. Transparency and Accountability Initiative (UNTAI), a Bush Administration program created by the U.S. Mission to the United Nations that tracks the adoption of management reforms by U.N. funds and programs.[26] Additionally, in September 2010, then-Assistant Secretary for International Organization Affairs (IO) Esther Brimmer announced that the IO Bureau hired an advisor on effectiveness, whose role is to "systematically review the effectiveness of international organizations," including U.N. entities.[27]

The Administration has generally resisted legislation tying U.S. contributions to specific U.N. reforms due to concerns that it may interfere with the President's ability to conduct diplomacy. In an April 2011 statement before the House Foreign Affairs Committee, then-U.S. Permanent Representative to the United Nations Susan Rice remarked that failing to pay U.N. dues "undermines [U.S.] credibility and influence [in the United Nations]—not just on reform, but on a range of U.S. national security policies."[28]

George W. Bush Administration

The George W. Bush Administration was an active participant in U.N. reform efforts. It identified several key priorities that it believed would help the United Nations improve its effectiveness, including (1) management, budget, and secretariat reform; (2) increased oversight and accountability; (3) review of all U.N. mandates and missions; and (4) fiscal discipline.

Prior to and after the adoption of the 2005 World Summit Outcome Document, the Bush Administration attempted to work with like-minded countries and the U.N. Secretary-General to move a reform agenda forward. Some reform initiatives supported by President Bush, particularly management and oversight reforms, were not approved or considered by the General Assembly. Administration officials expressed dissatisfaction with the overall effectiveness of some previously implemented reforms, as well as the pace of reform efforts. Nevertheless, the Administration did not support mandatory withholding of U.S. payments to the United Nations.

Reform Perspectives and Priorities

A significant challenge for advocates of U.N. reform is finding common ground among the disparate definitions of reform held by various stakeholders. There is no common definition of U.N. reform and, as a result, there is often debate over the scope, appropriateness, and effectiveness of past and current reform initiatives. One method for determining how a stakeholder defines U.N. reform may be to identify policy priorities in the U.N. reform debate. In some cases, common objectives among stakeholders have translated into substantive reform policy, though shared goals do not always guarantee successful outcomes.

The Secretary-General

On December 14, 2006, Ban Ki-moon of South Korea took the oath of office to succeed outgoing U.N. Secretary-General Kofi Annan. He was appointed to a second five-year term on June 21, 2011, and since his first term has stated that U.N. reform is one of his top priorities. He maintains that progress needs to be made in three areas: (1) improving what and how the United Nations delivers on the ground, (2) doing more with what the United Nations has, and (3) increasing accountability. During his tenure, Ban's reform efforts have included restructuring the Department of Field Support and the Department of Disarmament Affairs; establishing a "Change Management Team"[29] to address management issues and future reform efforts; and proposals to improve staff mobility.

The extent and effectiveness of Ban's reform efforts remain to be seen. On the one hand, some experts and policy makers argue that Ban is not doing enough to press member states for comprehensive reform or to institute reforms in the Secretariat. On the other hand, some emphasize that like previous Secretaries-General, Ban's success in achieving reform is limited by the responsibilities of his office. Although the Secretary-General—as the "chief administrative officer" of the United Nations—can facilitate and advocate reform, the power to implement wide-ranging and comprehensive change lies primarily with U.N. member states. Many of these states are concerned that reform activities initiated by the Secretary-General may undermine their authority. For example, the Secretary-General's aforementioned Change Management Team, which was supported by the

United States, has faced opposition from many developing countries due to such concerns.[30]

Developed and Developing Countries

Past reform debates in the U.N. General Assembly and its committees have drawn attention to fundamental differences that exist among some member states, particularly developing countries (represented primarily by the Group of 77),[31] and developed countries (particularly the United States, Japan, and members of the European Union). Developed countries, which account for the majority of assessed contributions to the U.N. regular budget, tend to focus on the United Nations' role in maintaining international peace and security and the overall efficiency of the organization. They would like the Secretary-General to have greater flexibility and authority to implement reforms, specifically those related to oversight and human resources. Generally, they make significantly larger financial contributions to the U.N. system than developing countries and therefore want to ensure that their funds are used in ways they perceive as most effective. Conversely, developing countries, which constitute the largest U.N. voting bloc, often focus on development-oriented policies. They generally object to reforms that would enhance the power of the Secretary-General and decrease the power of the General Assembly and its Fifth Committee (which addresses budget and administrative issues). In the past, some developing countries have expressed concern that reform initiatives might drain resources from development programs. They have also suggested that reforms proposed by the Secretary-General tend to be influenced by countries that are the largest financial contributors to the United Nations.

Many observers are concerned that the aforementioned difference in reform philosophy has created deadlocks in the General Assembly and significantly delayed the implementation of management and budget reforms. Such differences were highlighted in December 2005 when a group of U.N. member states, led primarily by developed countries such as the United States and Japan, sought to link the U.N. budget to progress on management reforms. The countries placed a spending cap of $950 million (about six months of U.N. spending) on the two-year, $3.6 billion budget in hopes that the General Assembly would adopt a series of management and budget reform measures proposed by then-Secretary-General Annan. On May 8, 2006, the General Assembly's Fifth Committee bypassed the traditional practice of budget-by-consensus and voted on a resolution, supported by the G-77, which approved some reforms but delayed the consideration of several others. The developed nations that imposed the budget cap were disappointed with the outcome. They eventually lifted the budget cap in June 2006 because they were unwilling to cause a shutdown of the United Nations.[32]

U.N. Reform-Related Commissions, Task Forces, and Groups

Since the United Nations was established in 1945, many commissions, panels, committees, and task forces (hereinafter referred to collectively as "groups") have been created to examine ways to improve the United Nations.[33] These groups are established by a variety of stakeholders, including past secretaries-general, individual member states, groups of member states, non-governmental organizations, academic institutions, and others. The following sections address the findings of a cross-section of these groups—the Volcker Commission, the U.S. Institute of Peace U.N. Reform Task Force, and then-Secretary-General Kofi Annan's 2005 report, *In Larger Freedom: Toward Development, Security, and Human Rights for All.*

Though the circumstances and mandates for each group are different, they made similar recommendations for improving the United Nations. Notably, each group highlighted the need for enhanced internal oversight and Secretariat reform, including staff buyouts and enhanced financial disclosure requirements.

The groups also emphasized the need for overall streamlining and consolidation of the U.N. system (see **Appendix B** for a side-by-side comparison of the recommendations).

The Volcker Commission

In April 2004, then-Secretary-General Annan, with the endorsement of the U.N. Security Council, appointed an independent high-level commission to inquire into corruption in the U.N.-led Iraq Oil-for-Food Program.[34] The commission, led by former U.S. Federal Reserve Chairman Paul Volcker, concluded that the failures of the Oil-For-Food Program were evidence of a greater need for "fundamental and wide-ranging administrative reform" in the United Nations.[35]

The commission recommended establishing an Independent Oversight Board to review U.N. auditing, accounting, and budgeting activities; creating the position of Chief Operating Officer to oversee administrative matters such as personnel and planning practices; providing fair compensation to third parties involved in U.N. programs (while ensuring that the compensation does not lead to inappropriate profit); and expanding financial disclosure requirements to cover a variety of U.N. staff, including those working on procurement.

U.S. Institute of Peace U.N. Reform Task Force

In December 2004, Congress directed the U.S. Institute of Peace to create a bipartisan task force to examine ways to improve the United Nations so that it is better equipped to meet modern-day security and human rights challenges.[36] Congress appropriated $1.5 million to the task force and required that it submit a report on its findings to the House Committee on Appropriations.[37]

The task force identified improving internal oversight as its single most important reform recommendation. It supported the creation of an independent oversight board to direct the budget and activities of the Office of Internal Oversight Services (OIOS). It also recommended several management reforms, including establishing the position of Chief Operating Officer, creating a U.N. Ethics Office, and enhancing whistle-blower protection. It supported broadening the U.N. staff financial disclosure policy, and recommended the review of all U.N. mandates five years or older, as well as the incorporation of sunset clauses into all new mandates. The task force supported incorporating results-based budgeting into the U.N. system, and a one-time buyout for all unwanted or unneeded staff. It recommended the creation of a new U.N. Human Rights Council to replace the discredited Commission on Human Rights, but was unable to come to consensus on Security Council reform.

Secretary-General Annan's Report, in Larger Freedom

On March 21, 2005, then-Secretary-General Annan released his report, *In Larger Freedom*, in response to the findings of the High-Level Panel on Threats, Challenges and Change.[38]

The report was presented to member states as a starting point for discussion at the 2005 U.N. World Summit, and included the following management reform recommendations:

- the review of all U.N. mandates over five years old;
- a one-time staff-buyout to ensure U.N. Secretariat staff meets current needs;

- the establishment of a cabinet-style decision-making body in the Secretariat to improve management and policy activities;
- the review of all budget and human resource operations; and
- a comprehensive review of Office of Internal Oversight Services to examine ways to enhance its authority and effectiveness.

In addition, Secretary-General Annan proposed a broad range of institutional and programmatic reforms, including modifying the composition of the U.N. Security Council so that it more adequately reflects current political realities, and replacing the Commission on Human Rights with a new Human Rights Council. Annan also recommended streamlining the General Assembly agenda and committee structure so that the Assembly can increase the speed of its decision-making and react more swiftly and efficiently to events as they occur.

MECHANICS OF IMPLEMENTING REFORM

Previous and current U.N. reform initiatives encompass an array of organizational issues that may require different processes for implementation. These reforms might be achieved by amending the U.N. Charter or through various non-Charter reforms. Charter amendment is a rarely used practice and has only occurred on three occasions. Non-Charter reforms are more common and comparatively easier to achieve.

Amending the U.N. Charter

Articles 108 and 109 of the U.N. Charter provide for potential changes to the document. Article 108 states that a proposed Charter amendment must be approved by two-thirds of the full General Assembly, and be ratified "according to the constitutional processes" of two-thirds of U.N. member states, including all permanent members of the Security Council.[39] The Charter was first amended in 1963 to increase U.N. Security Council membership from 11 to 15 members, and to increase the Economic and Social Council (ECOSOC) membership from 18 to 27. It was last amended in 1973, when ECOSOC membership increased from 27 to 54.[40]

Examples of possible reform initiatives that might involve amending the U.N. Charter include, but are not limited to, increasing permanent and/or nonpermanent Security Council membership; increasing membership on ECOSOC; and adding or removing a principal organ.[41]

Article 109 of the Charter allows for a convening of a General Conference of U.N. members with the purpose of "reviewing the present Charter." The date and place of the conference would be determined by a two-thirds vote in the General Assembly, and an affirmative vote from any nine Security Council members.

Potential revisions to the Charter would be adopted at the conference by a two-thirds vote (with each country having one vote), and take effect when ratified by the governments of two-thirds of U.N. member states. A Charter review conference has never been held.

Non-Charter Reform Process

Since 1945, the General Assembly has authorized reforms of its own processes and procedures— as well as those of the Secretariat—without Charter amendment. The General Assembly has established various fora for discussing reform issues, including a Committee on the Charter of the United Nations[42] and a Working Group on the Security Council.[43] The General Assembly has also implemented reforms on its own by adopting proposals introduced by member states or the Secretary-General.[44] The Secretary-General may also institute reform in his capacity as chief administrative officer, as well as make administrative decisions regarding the organization of some U.N. departments. Secretary-General Ban, for example, restructured the Departments of Field Support and Disarmament Affairs and established a Change Management Team to consider possible future reform efforts. Other non-Charter reforms have included the establishment of consensus-based budgeting in 1986; the creation of an Office of Strategic Planning in the Secretariat authorized by Secretary-General Annan in 1997; and the establishment of a Peacebuilding Commission by the Security Council and General Assembly in 2006.[45]

LOOKING AHEAD: POSSIBLE CHALLENGES TO REFORM

Achieving meaningful and comprehensive U.N. reform is a significant and ongoing challenge for U.N. member states. The 113th Congress may wish to take possible reform obstacles into account when considering legislation that exercises oversight or supports a reform agenda.

National Self-Interest and Differing Reform Perspectives

Each U.N. member state has its own political agenda and foreign policy goals, and may also have its own definition of U.N. reform. As a result, member states often hold differing views on when reform is necessary, how best to implement reform, and how to measure the success or failure of a given reform initiative.

In some cases, failure to reach consensus can lead to significant delay, or failure, of certain reform initiatives. Some member states package their policy priorities as U.N. reform to further their own policy goals. This can cause distrust among member states as countries question whether reform proposals by other member states are based on self-interest or a genuine desire to improve the U.N. system.

Competing Priorities

Some observers cite the inability of U.N. member states or secretaries-general to effectively prioritize reform initiatives as an obstacle to U.N. reform. When Secretary-General Annan presented reform proposals in 2005, for example, he requested that they be adopted by the General Assembly not in increments, but as a package of reforms.[46] Instead of considering a large series of reform proposals, some observers argue that member states should select only a few reform priorities and work toward their adoption and implementation.

Others contend that the most efficient way to achieve reform may be for member states first to adopt reform initiatives they can agree to and then gradually work toward tackling the more divisive and complicated reform issues.

Organizational Structure and Bureaucracy

The United Nations is a highly complex and decentralized organization, and therefore may be slow to consider or implement potential reforms. Some argue that there is a "culture of inaction"[47] in the United Nations, and that U.N. managers and staff are resistant to the implementation of new programs, changes to existing programs, and modifications to staffing and personnel policies.

Many contend that prospective and agreed-to reforms lack clear plans for implementation, including deadlines and cost estimates. They stress that this overall lack of planning may affect the progress and ultimate success of reforms already implemented, as well as those reforms currently being considered by the General Assembly. Some also emphasize that without proper implementation plans and follow-up, U.N. member states may be unable to adequately gauge the overall effectiveness of reforms.

Limited Resources

Many observers note that a significant challenge for U.N. reform efforts may be the effective implementation of reforms within the current U.N. budget. Some reform initiatives are established by member states to operate "within existing resources." Many argue that the existing U.N. budget limits may not be able to support all of the reform initiatives currently being considered. Some member states, including the United States, however, contend that money saved from other reforms could create a funding source for further reforms and/or the creation of new U.N. programs or bodies.

External Influences

The complex relationships that exist among member states outside of the U.N. system may be another challenge affecting U.N. reform efforts. These relationships are entirely independent of the United Nations but can affect how countries work together within the U.N. framework to achieve reform objectives. Military conflict, religious and ethnic differences, political conflict, trade and economic issues, and geography can all potentially impact reform priorities and cooperation among U.N. member states.

APPENDIX A. PREVIOUS REFORM LEGISLATION

When considering U.N. reform issues, Congress may wish to explore the nature and effectiveness of past legislative approaches and the extent to which they may have influenced the adoption of reform measures at the United Nations. There is some evidence that legislation such as the Kassebaum-Solomon Amendment and the Helms-Biden Agreement may have led, either directly or indirectly, to substantive changes in U.N. policies. The following sections highlight selected reform legislation from 1986 to the present and note any subsequent changes to internal U.N. policy.

Kassebaum-Solomon Amendment (1986-1987)[48]

In the mid-1980s, some Members of Congress expressed concern that U.S. influence over the U.N. budget was not proportionate to its rate of assessment. In 1986 Congress passed legislation, popularly known as the "Kassebaum-Solomon amendment," which required that the U.S. assessed contribution to the U.N. regular budget be reduced to 20% unless the United Nations gave major U.N. financial contributors a greater say in the budget process.[49] Subsequently, in 1986 the General Assembly adopted a new budget and planning process that incorporated consensus-based budgeting as a decision-making mechanism, thus giving member states with higher assessment levels a potentially greater voice in the budget process.

U.N. Office of Internal Oversight Services (1993)

In the early 1990s, some Members of Congress and the Administration were concerned with the apparent lack of oversight and accountability within the U.N. system. In 1993, as part of the FY1994 State Department Appropriations Act, Congress directed that 10% of U.S. assessed contributions to the U.N. regular budget be withheld until the Secretary of State certified to Congress that "the United Nations has established an independent office with responsibilities and powers substantially similar to offices of Inspectors General Act of 1978."[50] On July 29, 1994, the U.N. General Assembly established the Office of Internal Oversight Services (OIOS) which reports directly to the Secretary-General and provides "internal auditing, investigation, inspection, programme monitoring, evaluation and consulting services to all U.N. activities under the Secretary-General's authority."[51]

Helms-Biden Agreement (1999)

In the late 1990s, Congress and the Administration negotiated and agreed to legislation that would further U.S. reform policy at the United Nations. The Helms-Biden bill authorized payment of some U.S. arrears if specific reform benchmarks were met and certified to Congress by the Secretary of State.[52] Under the terms of Helms-Biden, the United States agreed to (1) pay $819 million in arrearages over fiscal years 1998, 1999, and 2000; and (2) forgive $107 million owed to the United States by the United Nations in peacekeeping costs if the United Nations applied the $107 million to U.S. peacekeeping arrears. For arrearage payments to occur, Congress required that the U.S. assessment for contributions to the U.N. regular budget be reduced from 25% to 22% and that the peacekeeping contribution be reduced from 30% to 25%.[53] In December 2000, the U.N. General Assembly reduced the regular budget assessment level to from 25% to 22%, and the Peacekeeping share from approximately 30.4% to 28%. In subsequent years, the U.S. peacekeeping assessment continued to fall and is now close to 26.5%.

Appendix B. Key U.N. Reform Recommendations and Proposals by Independent and U.N. Affiliated Groups

Report of the Task Force on the United Nations (June 2004, December 2005)	In Larger Freedom: Towards Development, Security and Human Rights for All (March 2005)	Report of the Independent Inquiry Committee into the United Nations Oil-for-Food Program (October 2005)
Improved management reform, including:	Secretariat reform, including:	Strengthen U.N. management practices, including:

Appendix B. (Continued)

Establish an Independent Oversight Board to function as an independent audit committee;	Review of the Office of Internal Oversight Services and general strengthening of internal oversight;	Establish an Independent Oversight Board with responsibility over internal and external audits and investigations;
Establish the role of Chief Operating Officer (COO);	Creation of a cabinet-style decision-making mechanism;	Create the position of Chief Operating Officer (COO);
Establish policies for improved financial disclosure standards, whistle-blower protection; and	Authority/resources for Secretary-General to realign and/or buy-out Secretariat staff; and full review of budget and human resources operations; and	Expand financial disclosure requirements for U.N. staff, including the Secretary-General, Deputy-Secretary-General, and those involved in procurement and/or disbursement;
Review of all U.N. mandates and sunset clauses for new mandates.	Review of all U.N. mandates five years or older.	Improve coordination and framework for cross-agency U.N. programs; and
Reorganization of the General Assembly;	Streamlining the General Assembly to speed-up decision-aking processes;	Ensure third party agencies involved in U.N. programs are entitled to fair compensation.
Replace the Commission on Human Rights with a new Human Rights Council;	Replace the discredited Commission on Human Rights with a new Human Rights Council;	
Identification of U.N. programs that could be more effective if funded by voluntary contributions; and	Modify composition of the Security Council to reflect current political realities; and	
Improving the Department of Peacekeeping Operations so that it becomes "a more independent program" with its own rules and regulations to address its unique mission.	Reform ECOSOC so it may better coordinate the U.N. development agenda and guide other economic and social agencies in the United Nations.	

APPENDIX C. ORGANIZATIONAL CHART OF THE U.N. SYSTEM

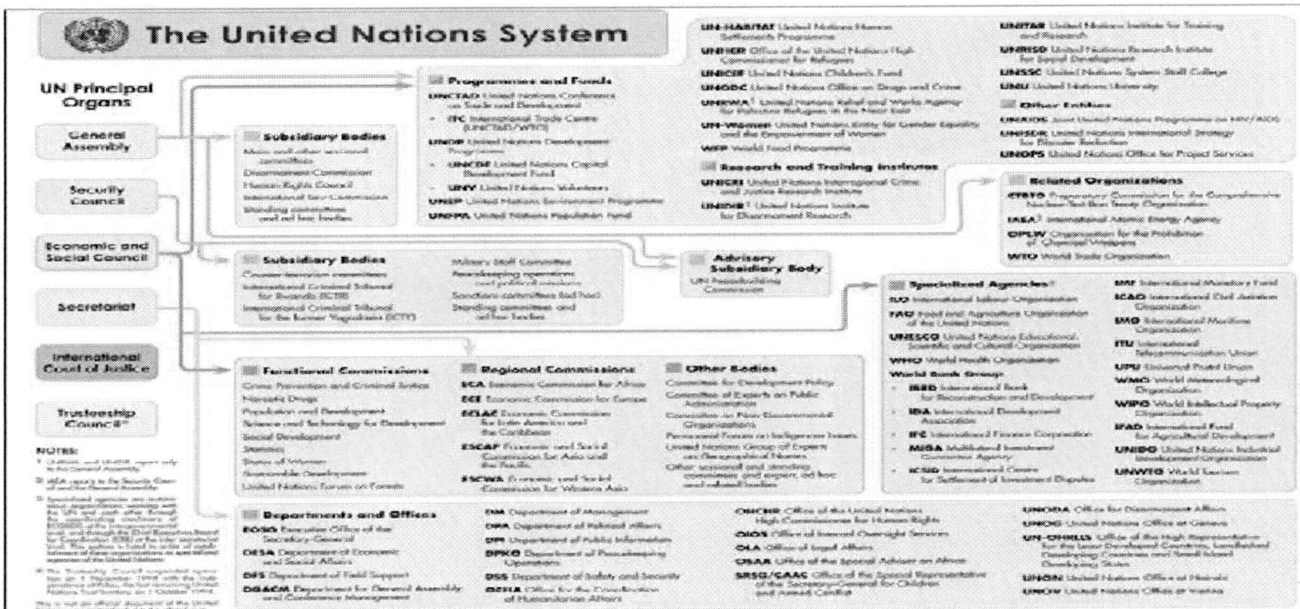

Source: United Nations.

End Notes

[1] U.N. membership grew from 51 countries in 1945, to 114 countries in 1963. Currently, the United Nations has 193 member states. Amendments to the Charter related to increased membership are discussed in the "Mechanics of Implementing Reform" section of this report.

[2] For more information on this group and other U.N. reform efforts prior to the 1980s, see "Reforming the United Nations: Lessons from a History in Progress," by Edward C. Luck, *Academic Council on the United Nations System— Occasional Papers Series*, 2003.

[3] In 1986, under pressure from the United States and other industrialized countries, the General Assembly established a high-level group of 18 intergovernmental experts to "review the efficiency of the administrative and financial functioning" of the United Nations. The group made 71 recommendations to the General Assembly, including a revised budgetary process that introduced the use of consensus-based budgeting. The group of experts was convened, in part, because of U.S. legislation popularly known as the "Kassebaum-Solomon Amendment," which directed that U.S. contributions to the U.N. regular budget be reduced if countries making the largest financial contributions did not have a more substantial influence in the U.N. budget process. See **Appendix A** for more information on KassebaumSolomon and other U.N. reform-related legislation.

[4] Statement by Ambassador Rosemary DiCarlo in the General Assembly Plenary Debate on the Security Council Annual Report and Reform, New York, November 15, 2012.

[5] The Summit convened to review the progress made in the fulfillment of the 2000 Millennium Summit goals and commitments made in other earlier U.N. conferences. The 2000 Millennium Summit was held from September 6-8, 2000, in New York.

[6] U.N. document, A/RES/60/1, *2005 World Summit Outcome*, September 16, 2005.

[7] Mandates are resolutions adopted by members of each of the principal U.N. organs. (The six U.N. organs are the General Assembly, Security Council, Trusteeship Council, Economic and Social Council, International Court of Justice, and Secretariat.) Mandates can be both conceptual and specific; they can establish or interpret international norms, provide policy direction on substantive and/or administrative issues, or request conferences, activities, operations and reporting requirements.

[8] For more information on the Council, see CRS Report RL33608, *The United Nations Human Rights Council: Issues for Congress*, by Luisa Blanchfield.

[9] U.N. document, A/RES/61/261, April 4, 2007.

[10] For more information on U.N. reform activities, see the U.N. Secretariat Department of Management website at http://www.un.org/en/hq/dm/.

[11] For example, Congress has enacted laws supporting U.N. policies and/or requiring that U.N. member states comply with U.N. Security Council resolutions or the directives of other U.N. bodies, such as the General Assembly and Human Rights Council.

[12] For more information, see CRS Report R42999, *The United Nations Educational, Scientific, and Cultural Organization (UNESCO)*, by Luisa Blanchfield and Marjorie Ann Browne.

[13] For more information, see CRS Report RL34074, *The Palestinians: Background and U.S. Relations*, by Jim Zanotti.

[14] For a more detailed examination of U.S. funding of the United Nations, see CRS Report RL33611, *United Nations System Funding: Congressional Issues*, by Marjorie Ann Browne.

[15] Section 307 of the Foreign Assistance Act of 1961 (P.L. 87-195; 22 U.S.C. 2227), as amended.

[16] The U.N. regular budget funds core U.N. activities for the General Assembly, Security Council, and other U.N. bodies. It also supports human rights-related activities; staffing and administration at U.N. headquarters, funding and staffing for international conferences, and special political missions, among other things.

[17] October 21, 2011 letter from Ronald Weich, Assistant Attorney General, U.S. Department of Justice, to then-HFAC Chairperson Rep. Ileana Ros-Lehtinen.

[18] Foreign Affairs Authorization Act for FY1994 and 1995 (P.L. 103-236), April 30, 1994. On September 30, 2002, Congress lifted the 25% cap on the peacekeeping assessment to allow the United States to pay its current assessments (P.L. 107-228, §402).

[19] Additionally, some observers contend that if the United States were to delay or stop payment of its arrears, it may risk losing its vote in the General Assembly—a generally undesirable outcome for many Members of Congress and the Administration. In 1999, for example, the United States came very close to losing its General Assembly vote. Under Article 19 of the U.N. Charter, a U.N. member state with arrears equaling or exceeding the member state's assessments for the two preceding years will have no vote in the General Assembly.

[20] "The Right Approach to Achieving U.N. Reform," Better World Campaign, *Better World Campaign Fact Sheet.*

[21] Most recently, Christopher Burnham served as U.N. Under-Secretary for Management. He stepped down before Secretary-General Annan's term ended in 2007. Prior to Christopher Burnham, the post was held by Catherine Bertini, also a U.S. citizen. The current Under-Secretary-General for Management is Yukio Takasu of Japan.

[22] In the 1970s and 1980s, for example, the "Geneva Group" was formed to encourage dialogue and cooperation among like-minded U.N. member states. It was composed mostly of Western countries that were the United Nations' largest financial contributors. The group focused mainly on financial and budgetary issues, and some contend it was instrumental in bringing about budgetary restraint in some of the U.N. specialized agencies. For more information, see *The United States and Multilateral Institutions,* edited by Margaret P. Karns and Karen A. Mingst, Unwin Hyman Publishers, 1990, p. 313; and *United Nations: Law, Policies and Practice,* edited by Rudiger Wolfrum, Martinus Nijhoff Publishers, 1995, pp. 70-71.

[23] See (1) Remarks by the President to the United Nations General Assembly, September 23, 2009, White House Press Office, and (2) Remarks by Ambassador Esther Brimmer delivered at the Brookings Institution, "Revitalizing the United Nations and Multilateral Cooperation: The Obama Administration's Progress," February 1, 2011.

[24] During the George W. Bush Administration, the U.S. Permanent Representative to the United Nations reported to the Secretary of State. During the Clinton Administration, the Permanent Representative reported to the President.

[25] Drawn from statements by Administration officials, including statement of then Ambassador Susan E. Rice to the House Foreign Affairs Committee for a hearing entitled, "U.S. Policy Toward the United Nations," April 7, 2011; U.S. Mission to the United Nations, Statement on Transparency Initiatives at the U.N. by then-Ambassador Torsella, September 14, 2011; State Department Fact Sheet, Advancing U.S. Interests at the United Nations, September 25, 2012; State Department Fact Sheet: Conclusion of the 67th General Assembly Session of the Fifth Committee, December 28, 2012; and Remarks by Ambassador Samantha Power, U.S. Permanent Representative to the United Nations, at the Fifth Committee on the Final Budget Report for 2012-2013, December 16, 2013.

[26] In 2011, the Obama Administration launched the second phase of UNTAI (UNTAI-II) to identify areas where member states can increase oversight and accountability to ensure their contributions are used efficiently and effectively.

[27] The effectiveness advisor also promotes "rigorous evaluation standards that the organizations themselves can take up, to expand their own capacity for self-improvement." See Remarks by then-Assistant Secretary Brimmer to the American Foreign Service Association, "The Role and Relevance of Multilateral Diplomacy in U.S. Foreign Policy," January 11, 2011.

[28] Statement of then-Ambassador Susan E. Rice to the House Foreign Affairs Committee for a hearing entitled "U.S. Policy Toward the United Nations," April 7, 2011.

[29] Ban appointed Assistant Secretary-General Atul Khare of India to lead the Change Management Team (CMT) in May 2011. The CMT published its recommendations in December 2011 at http://www.un.org/sg/pdf/the-changeplan.pdf.

[30] For an overview of member state perspectives on this issue, see U.N. Department of Public Information document GA/11222, April 9, 2012. Also see U.S. Mission to the United Nations, "Statement by Ambassador Joseph Torsella, U.S. Representative for U.N. Management and Reform, on Action Taken on Fifth Committee Resolutions from the First Resumed Session of the 66th GA, General Assembly," April 9, 2012.

[31] Comprised of 133 members, the Group of 77 of (G-77) is the largest intergovernmental organization of developing countries in the United Nations.

[32] On July 7, 2006, the General Assembly approved the reforms recommended by the Fifth Committee. See U.N. document, A/RES/60/283, July 7, 2006.

[33] For a discussion on the effectiveness of various U.N. reform groups, see keynote speech at University of Waterloo made by Edward C. Luck, Director of the Center on International Organization at Columbia University, "U.N. Reform Commissions: Is Anyone Listening?" May 16, 2002.

[34] U.N. document, A/RES/1538, April 21, 2004. The Committee was chaired by Paul Volcker and included Professor Mark Peith of Switzerland, an expert on money laundering from the Organization for Economic Cooperation and Development (OECD); and Justice Richard Goldstone of South Africa, a former prosecutor with the International Criminal Tribunals for the former Yugoslavia and Rwanda. The Commission's final report was released on October 27, 2005.

[35] "Briefing by Paul A. Volcker Chairman of the Independent Inquiry Committee into the U.N. Oil-For-Food Program for the Permanent Subcommittee on Investigations of the U.S. Senate," Washington, DC, October 31, 2005.

[36] Consolidated Appropriations Act, 2005 (P.L. 108-447, December 8, 2004). In the report accompanying the act, conferees stated that they were "deeply troubled by the inaction of the United Nations on many fronts, especially in regard to the genocide in Darfur, Sudan and the allegations of corruption regarding the United Nations Oil-For-Food Program." Conferees directed that the task force should include experts from the American Enterprise Institute, Brookings Institution, Council on Foreign Relations, Center for Strategic and International Studies, Hoover Institution, and the Heritage Foundation.

[37] The Task Force was co-chaired by former Speaker of the House Newt Gingrich and former Senate Majority Leader George Mitchell, and released its first report, *American Interests and U.N. Reform* in June 2005. Following the 2005 U.N. World Summit in New York, the Task Force released an updated report entitled, *The Imperative for Action,* in December 2005.

[38] The 2005 World Summit Outcome Document called on the Secretary-General to improve U.N. system-wide coherence and coordination by "strengthening linkages" between the U.N.

system's normative work and its operational activities. Accordingly, in February 2006, the Secretary-General announced the creation of a High-Level Panel on System-wide Coherence to examine how the U.N. system can work more effectively, especially in the areas of development, humanitarian assistance, and the environment. The panel's final report emphasized the overall value and progress of the United Nations, but also noted that without substantial reforms the United Nations will be "unable to deliver on its promises and maintain its legitimate position at the heart of the multilateral system."

[39] Article 108 of the U.N. Charter states, "Amendments to the present Charter shall come into force for all Members of the United Nations when they have been adopted by a vote of two-thirds of the members of the General Assembly and ratified in accordance with their respective constitutional processes by two thirds of the members of the United Nations, including all the permanent members of the Security Council."

[40] Simma, Bruno, *The Charter of the United Nations: A Commentary*. Second Edition, Vol. II. New York, Oxford University Press, 2002, p. 1367-1357.

[41] Principal organs of the United Nations include the Trusteeship Council (TC); Security Council; General Assembly; Economic and Social Council; International Court of Justice; and the Secretariat. There is an ongoing effort to abolish the TC, a system that was designed to administer and supervise U.N. trust territories. The TC suspended its operations on November 1, 1994, with the independence of its last trust territory, Palau.

[42] The "Special Committee on the Charter of the United Nations and on the Strengthening of the Role of the Organization," was established in 1974 to consider "any specific proposals that Governments might make with a view to enhancing the ability of the U.N. to achieve its purposes," as well as "suggestions for the more effective functioning of the U.N. that might not require amendments to the Charter." The Committee also makes recommendations for possible Charter amendments. Most recently, in 1995 it proposed an amendment to delete "enemy state" clauses in the Charter.

[43] The "Working Group on the Question of Equitable Representation on and Increase in the Membership of the Security Council and Other Matters Related to the Security Council," was established in 1993.

[44] For example, in March 2006 the Assembly negotiated and approved a resolution replacing the previous U.N. Commission on Human Rights with a new Human Rights Council.

[45] An example of a possible non-Charter reform could be the redistribution of regional seats on the Security Council or ECOSOC. For further discussion on possible non-Charter reforms, see article by Louis B. Sohn, "Important Improvements in the Functioning of the Principal Organs of the United Nations that Can be Made Without Charter Revision," *American Journal of International Law,* October 1997.

[46] "The Secretary-General's Statement to the General Assembly," New York, March 21, 2005.

[47] "Annan's 'Culture of Inaction.'" *The Chicago Tribune,* December 12, 2006.

[48] For a more detailed account of the Kassebaum-Solomon Provisions, see CRS Report RL33611, *United Nations System Funding: Congressional Issues*, by Marjorie Ann Browne.

[49] Foreign Relations Authorization Act, FY1986 and 1987 (H.R. 2068, P.L. 99-93), Section 143, August 16, 1985.

[50] U.S. Department of State Appropriations Act, 1994 (H.R. 2519, P.L. 103-121), October 27, 1993.

[51] More information on OIOS is available at http://www.un.org/depts/oios/. See U.N. document, A/RES/48/218 B, August 12, 1994, for a detailed description of its mandate.

[52] The Helms-Biden Agreement was incorporated into the Consolidated Appropriations Act for FY2000 (H.R. 3194, P.L. 106-113), November 19, 1999.

[53] See archived CRS Report RL33700, *United Nations Peacekeeping: Issues for Congress*, by Marjorie Ann Browne, for further information.

INDEX

C

D

G

H

I

J

K

L

M

N

O

P

Q

R

S

T

U

V

W

Y